Zen
and
the
Practice
of
Teaching
English

Robert Tremmel

Boynton/Cook Publishers
HEINEMANN
Portsmouth, NH

For Michelle

Boynton/Cook Publishers, Inc.
A subsidiary of Reed Elsevier Inc.
361 Hanover Street
Portsmouth, NH 03801–3912
http://www.boyntoncook.com

Offices and agents throughout the world

©1999 by Robert Tremmel

The author and publisher wish to thank those who have generously given permission to reprint borrowed material:

Portions of the book are adapted from "Zen and the Art of Reflective Practice in Teacher Education" by Robert Tremmel. From *Harvard Educational Review,* 63: 434–488, 1993.

"Your First Time Driving the Milford Blacktop" by Robert Tremmel originally appeared in *Driving the Milford Blacktop.* It is reprinted here with permission of *BkMk Press* and the Curators of the University of Missouri–Kansas City.

Library of Congress Cataloging-in-Publication Data

Tremmel, Robert, 1948–
    Zen and the practice of teaching english / Robert Tremmel
        p.   cm.
    Includes bibliographical references.
    ISBN 0-86709-480-X
    1. Teaching.   2. Tremmel, Robert, 1948–   .   3. Teachers—United States.
I. Title.
LB1025.3.T74   1999
371.102—dc21   98-48856
                                                                                    CIP

Editor: William Varner
Production: Elizabeth Valway
Cover design: Joni Doherty Design
Manufacturing: Louise Richardson

Printed in the United States of America on acid-free paper
03   02   01   00   99   DA   1   2   3   4   5

Contents

Acknowledgments

I remember sitting in the late Dick Hootman's office years ago at the University of Iowa complaining about some trouble I was having with my dissertation. Without waiting for me to finish, Hootman looked me in the eye and said, "Tremmel, shut up, quit whining, get the hell out of my office, and get to work."

Every teacher who has ever written a book about teaching knows from the beginning that without his or her teachers there would be nothing to say and nothing would ever get done. I want to thank Dick Hootman and all my teachers, wherever they are and wherever I have studied with them—from the living room to the classroom to the zendo, from the tailgate of an eighteen-wheeler to the handle of a hammer, from Tootsie's Orchid Lounge to the Flint Hills of Kansas to the North Inlet. In the same breath I also want to thank my students, many of whom, despite my initial dimwittedness, have turned out to be my best teachers. I especially want to thank those teachers, colleagues, and students who allowed me to use their words, written and spoken, in this book.

I also want to thank the editors of BkMk Press, *Poetry Northwest,* and the *Harvard Educational Review* for permission to reprint previously published material.

I am particularly grateful to these individuals: Peter Stillman, who gave me the initial encouragement I needed to pursue this task; Bill Varner and Mary Rose O'Reilley, two tough, kind readers; Dale Ross and Tom Kent, two department chairs who lead from the heart; Dan Royer, of Grand Valley State University, who gave me important guidance in the early going; Dave Steffen, who opened the door of a classroom without doors; and Georgiana Peet Miller of Ithaca, Michigan, who has spent a lifetime treating wanderers from strange lands with kindness.

And my deepest appreciation goes to Michelle Tremmel, who, for reasons I do not entirely understand, was willing to join me in this and all the efforts and joys of life and practice.

Prologue

I am a teacher. I come from a family of teachers. My mother was a music teacher. Her first job was in a rural school at a place called Buck Creek, Iowa, back in the 1930s. A few years ago, in the winter, I drove through Buck Creek on my way to somewhere else. There was a tired-looking school building on the east side of the blacktop, some houses, old foundations, and pasture land flowing out from the road and spreading on either side of the creek. It had a harsh feel to it, almost wild and hostile, and I was glad to be passing on rather than staying.

Though teaching is in my blood, it does not reside easily or peacefully there. Despite the fact that I have been a teacher for the better part of twenty-five years, comfort and self-satisfaction have always eluded me, and the nature of my profession has always puzzled me. For much of that time I was quite willing to ignore my doubts, though, and go about my business, hoping that even if I did not know exactly what I was doing, if I did the best I could and avoided calling attention to myself, the universe would ignore me and not force me to confront what I feared I could never understand.

But there was one thing I did not know about the universe: no matter how long it might seem willing to ignore you, eventually your turn will come. When that happens, it is no longer possible to continue to overlook or be nonchalant about puzzlements and fears. And so several years ago I reached a point where the questions I had left unasked, and the deep-down discomforts I had tried to ignore, finally presented themselves to me in a way that demanded attention. Finally, I had no choice but to face my own ignorance and try to come to terms with what I had to admit I did not know about the profession I practiced each day.

This is not to say that I was ever lacking for places to seek wisdom about teaching. As long as I can remember, it has been as it is today: libraries have thousands of books and journals about teaching, textbook companies have series after series of materials, and on most university campuses there is an education professor every ten yards or so who is willing to give a lecture or organize a seminar at the slightest show of interest. Many of these professors, in fact, graciously shared large quantities of their knowledge with me, but somehow that was never quite enough of what it was I really needed.

Consequently, my purpose in writing this book is not to add to what I see as an already more than healthy and growing supply of scholarship about teaching. Instead, I want to focus on what I finally found in my own teaching practice that helped me start making sense of the confusion that was my own, but that I know is felt also by others who have teaching in their blood. Since I work every day with methods students on campus and student teachers in the schools, I am most accustomed to speaking to beginning teachers, and this book is primarily intended for them. However, since this book contains the voices and lives of many teachers with many years behind them, I hope what is in it might be something that experienced teachers will find valuable too.

In many ways this is a personal book based on personal knowledge I have managed to build up over a long stretch of years, and much of what I have to say is hard to locate in the official Ph.D.-sanctioned knowledge base for teaching. But this book is not isolated in its own world either. It reaches out and rests on three important grounding points that in many ways define for me the foundation of my life as a teacher. The first of these is the school. In one way or other everything I have to say in this book is based on my daily work with students, student teachers, and teachers in the secondary schools. Even though I teach at the university, the school is where the primary focus of my teaching practice rests and where I spend my most important teaching hours.

The second grounding point for me is professional knowledge. While I am not interested in adding weight to the scholarly corpus, I am not interested in ignoring it either: no one can live fully as a professional without maintaining contact with and participating in the ongoing conversation of other professionals. The era of educational history we inhabit right now is richly populated with a multitude of diverse groups and schools of thought—expressivists, cognitivists, Marxists, constructionists, postmodernists, neo-pragmatists, teacher researchers, and ethnographers, to name only a few. Some of these folks I refer directly to; many more hang in the background providing shape, color, and context for my own experience.

The third grounding point is harder to define than personal knowledge or professional knowledge—and much harder to talk about. For want of a better term, I think of it as spiritual knowledge, which each day I become more and more aware of not only as a dimension of teaching practice but of all the practices of living, from washing a dish, to planting a seed, to writing a book, to wading out into a fast-moving stream on an early spring day. How exactly I became interested in this side of things is not entirely clear to me, but much of it I believe has to do with the steady contact I have had with Zen texts and Zen teachers in the Midwest since the early 1980s.

I know that there are many who believe that spiritual practice in general, and Zen practice in particular, should occupy no part of serious discussions about teaching. I also know that there are some of my colleagues around the country who have objected to earlier writing I have done in this area. Believe me, I take these objections seriously. I have no difficulty at all sympathizing with the reluctance of anyone to find relevance in something so apparently foreign as Zen, and there have been times I have been close to abandoning this project. The sense of it I have come to finally, though, is that English education as a discipline and teaching as a profession have generally been strengthened in times when we have been able to open our eyes and minds toward what seems new and different, and that the broader our commitment to diversity, the better off we will be and the better able to serve our students.

And Zen is nothing if it is not diverse. Anyone who has been in the "Eastern Thought" section of a bookstore lately knows that Zen means many things to many people—from basketball coaches to physicists, to believers in some kind of "new age." For me, however, Zen is quintessentially old age—it is ancient—and comes down to my own personal experiences with it, which begin and end most days on the traditional meditation cushions used in Japanese monasteries and Zen centers in this country. But it does not end there: what happens—or does not happen—on the cushions has a way of carrying over into all the thoughts and actions of each day. I have heard many teachers say it in many ways: "Zen life is everyday life; Zen mind is everyday mind." That is how it increasingly seems to me, and, increasingly, for me the distance between spiritual life and everyday life, including professional life, seems to be shrinking.

In this respect, Zen, among the world's spiritual disciplines, is not unique. I cannot imagine how anyone could seriously follow any religious or devotional path without trying to live it fully, moment by moment, breath by breath throughout the activities of each day. So, while Zen provides a key point of reference for me in making sense of living and teaching, I am under no illusion that it is in any way a special or particularly compelling point of reference: it is simply my point of reference. That is all. At the same time I also am under no illusion that I have attained any sort of personal enlightenment or wisdom that qualifies me to speak authoritatively about Zen. No matter how Zen may or may not affect the way I live my life, my practice and my understanding are just what they are. My degrees are in English and English Education. If you want to become a great sage or achieve great enlightenment, do not bother with this book. Go find a great master. If you want to live the teacher's life, though, this book of mine may have something for you.

"The real cycle you're working on is a cycle called yourself. The machine that appears to be 'out there' and the person that appears to be 'in here' are not two separate things."
—Robert Pirsig, *Zen and the Art of Motorcycle Maintenance*

Chapter One

Beginning with Failure

In order to find a point from which to begin I need to go back and tell something of my life as a teacher. This is not easy for me because in order to do it, I need to begin with failure—two failures really—and let me say now they are not pretty.

The first failure came as a high school English teacher. This is an especially difficult confession to start off with, not only because failure is painful in itself, but because most books by teachers about teaching, whatever their purpose, begin with the author establishing credibility as a longtime and successful classroom teacher. I can make no such claim; it is a sorry fact that my twenty-five years as a teacher and teacher of teachers are carried on the very weak legs of a failed high school English teacher.

Second, I failed as a teacher educator, a failure I live with daily in my present job as a methods teacher, student teaching supervisor, and, believe it or not, coordinator of an English teacher preparation program. Talk about irony. From one perspective anyway, I am a perfect example of someone who, according to one of Murphy's Laws or Peter's Principles, has risen not only to the level of his incompetence, but has risen above it and become an administrator. This irony would be very discouraging if it were not so humorous, and if failure, in its many marvelous and illuminating forms, were not so essential to life, to the lifelong practice of teaching, and to the lifelong practice of living. But I am getting ahead of myself. This way of looking at things came to me much later. Best to return to the beginning.

Decision Making

All roads to failure, like all roads to success, begin with a decision. Like many young people in the turmoil of the late 1960s and early 1970s it took me until quite late in my undergraduate study to turn my attention toward the problem of what I should do when and if I grew up. For me, the arising of this particular problem coincided with finding myself in what, at the time, seemed like an unpromising situation:

- I was an English major.
- I was not a good student.
- The war in Vietnam was not going well and the Selective Service felt quite strongly that selecting me for service would help defeat the enemy (whoever that was).
- I was newly married with an infant daughter.

What to do? I decided to become a teacher.

The more I think about that decision, the more it seems to have been an act of complete delusion. I had absolutely no qualifications, no experience, and no personal or professional qualities that even remotely hinted I could teach. At the time, my primary area of expertise was loading, hauling, and unloading furniture for North American Van Lines. Looking back on it, my decision-making process seems very much like the scene in the movie *Butch Cassidy and the Sundance Kid* where Butch and Sundance are running from the posse and eventually reach a narrow precipice overlooking a deep chasm with a raging river at the bottom. With nowhere else to go they decide they must jump. Just before that, though, Sundance turns to Butch and says, "I just remembered, I can't swim." Butch replies, "That's OK, the fall will probably kill you."

Yet, I know it was not that simple for me no matter how it may seem in retrospect. When I visit Washington, D.C. or the city park in my hometown, I see cut in stone the names of my classmates and neighbors, heroes I grew up with, and I get a clearer sense of how it was and what drove and complicated my decision: not just recklessness, but fear, ignorance, and shallowness; the desperation of those years; and my futile efforts to make sense of it all in the context of trying to choose a path for my life and the others in my life. It was not necessarily that I was truly pushed to the edge of nowhere like Butch Cassidy and the Sundance Kid, but it felt like it at the time, and no matter how many choices I might have had, I could not figure out which way to turn.

In a perfect and orderly world none of us would end up in situations like that. In a perfect and orderly world, making major life decisions would be a matter of using our rational, thinking minds and gifts of intelligence to select among clearly discernible alternatives. *A or B?* Should I do *this* or *that?* What are the *pros* and *cons?* Even in the imperfect world we actually live in we can often use these processes to make decisions.

But not always and not everyone every time. Sometimes the pressure of an important decision and our inability to understand what is happening can easily force our minds, like runaway motors, to rev out of control, overheat, and come near blowing. Instead of calmly and quietly weighing the alternatives, *A* or *B, pro* or *con,* our minds get suddenly loud and talky and raucous, and nothing seems clear. For me, the whole period of life during which I was deciding to become a teacher and then actually becoming one was not so much a reckless time as it was a noisy time—a time of unsettled mind. It was a time much like the time many of my students are going through right now, caught in their own confusions in the process of trying to decide whether or not to become teachers. Their noise was my noise. Exactly the same.

Into the R.W.

By the time my noisy mind and I graduated from college the war was winding down and the military was no longer interested in selecting me or anyone else, so I was free to enter what we liked then to call the R.W.: the Real World. Since there were few teaching jobs and too many teacher education graduates, I found only a few openings, applied a few places, and sent out a poorly constructed resume. My strongest effort, as I recall, was having the manager of the apartment complex where I was living at the time take a photo that showed me standing in front of a brick wall wearing a coat, a tie, and a vest. Nothing worked. Before I was even able to fail as a teacher, I failed at getting a teaching job.

Finally, I more or less resigned myself to the moving business by making a major career move from North American to Bekins Van Lines. If I could not succeed in my mischosen profession, at least I could help other people move from place to place in their quests for success. One morning when I was off the road and working in town, I was riding my bicycle to work through the university campus just as a summer rain shower broke out. Since I happened to be right outside the building where the educational placement office was, and since I had a small piece of unfinished business there, I decided to stop and let the rain pass over. When I got to the top of the stairs, dripping wet in my green Bekins uniform with the company logo on the sleeve, I saw the door of the placement office crack open. Out walked the director of placement, an incredibly intense woman with an impeccable sense of timing and a dramatic sense of humor. She was accompanied by a short, round man with bloodshot eyes who turned out to be the superintendent of a school district needing to hire an English teacher. The placement director took one look at me, rolled her eyes, grabbed my left arm and the superintendent's right arm, shoved us toward an interview room, and minutes later I became an English teacher.

The Wages of Decision Making

For years after, being a child of the 1960s with a sixties vocabulary, I liked to look back on that event as an immense "karmic" event that changed my life forever. I liked to think those storm clouds blew me out of the cab of a semi into the hands of the placement director with a single blast. This "karma" is an interesting word that requires some attention since it points toward an important dimension of living and making decisions. The word *karma* comes from the sanskrit and is used, as I used to use it, often and loosely here in the West. Many people like to say that it is "good karma" or "bad karma" when something extraordinary and unexpected happens to them. Most of the time I think what they really mean when they say that is they have been the beneficiary—or victim—of some gigantic coincidence. Others tend to link karma to ideas like "fate" or "chance" or even "Divine Providence." In *Shoeless Joe*, a novel about the reincarnation of the baseball player Shoeless Joe Jackson on a baseball diamond carved out of a cornfield, the author, W. P. Kinsella, has the main character say:

> It's the place and the time. The right place and right time. Iowa is the right place, and the time is right, too—a time when all the cosmic tumblers have clicked into place and the universe opens up for a few seconds, or hours, and shows you what is possible. (1982, 84)

Over the last several years, as I have come in contact with more and more teachers who have trained in Japanese monasteries, I have made some changes in my understanding of karma. The way I see it now, karma has less in common with concepts like fate than it does with what I remember as a fundamental law of physics, which states that for every action there is a reaction. This is a very commonsensical view of karma. It means that when one thing happens it causes something else to happen. If I do something, like plant a seed in the garden, something else will happen as a result of that: a stalk of corn will grow; which will bear an ear; which I will pick, boil a few minutes, put butter, salt, and pepper on; and which I will then eat, always moving left to right like a typewriter across the page, from the narrow end to the base.

In *Returning to Silence*, a book by Dainin Katagiri, a Zen teacher who died a few years ago, the definition of *karma* in the glossary says:

Action; result or effect of action. The doctrine that one's present experience is a product of previous actions and volitions, and that future
conditions depend on what one does in the present. (1988, 181)

This definition, like the law of physics, seems straightforward. It makes
each individual, and not some outside force, responsible for actions and
consequences. It is tricky, though, because we do not always know
what the result of an action might be and exactly what the action might
lead to or what will happen as a consequence. All we know is that
each time we do something, something else will happen as a result of
it. In this view of karma, what we do—both the big actions and small
actions—becomes very important. Taking the action of becoming a
teacher is particularly significant. From the very beginning a teacher's
life touches and has an impact on hundreds, even thousands of people:
colleagues, students, students' families, the communities that teachers
work in. This creates a burden of responsibility that often is very heavy
to bear. Along with the burden, though, come infinite possibilities.

One thing I learned as a result of my decision to become a teacher—
and from my subsequent failure—was that one should not, as I did,
make the decision to become a teacher either recklessly or in a state of
noisy confusion. My jump-and-swim action, the actions I took in the
rainstorm, and my actions in the interview room had widespread, un-
foreseen consequences for many people, especially me. At the beginning of my first year, I found myself teaching five sections and four
preparations of high school English in a six-period day, coaching the
speech students, and directing the all-school play for a total salary of
$7,000. In addition, the first week of school our first-year principal had
a great idea. He called me into his office and said, "We should have a
school page in the local newspaper to generate good publicity for the
school, and the new English teacher should be in charge. Figure out
how to do it!"

I was in a fix. I was a run-of-the-mill truck driver with a very lib-
eral education, was not yet close to discovering a commitment to teach,
and I was right in the middle of the most difficult of first-year teaching
situations. Even worse, nothing I had learned in my methods courses
or in my student teaching seemed to have prepared me for anything
that was happening. I am not saying that what I learned in college was
of no use. On the contrary, it was very useful and had taught me all
kinds of things about my discipline and about teaching. But it did not
teach me whatever it was I needed to succeed in the job I had. Even
when I finally made contact with a good language arts consultant at the
Area Education Agency, her ideas—which sounded great to me—were
completely at odds with the ideas of the principal, a man who was on
the spot himself, coping with a new job while working feverishly to
finish work on his Ph.D. so he could move on to a better job.

These were the circumstances of my first teaching job. I was a displaced person with no clear vision of what I wanted to do or why. I had no conscious sense of the life I wanted to live. I do not think that at the time I was even fully aware that it was possible to live a life rather than be lived by it. I was out of touch with many members of the community. I clumsily tried to use a student-centered approach that was out of touch with the administration and most of the other teachers. I resisted using the textbooks that would have made my job easier and my work more acceptable. I had more preparations than I could handle. I was not very good at discipline and classroom management. (The going-away gift one student gave me on the last day of school was a joint of marijuana the size of a pocket flashlight wrapped up in colored paper and ribbons.) Everything was in place for failure, and that is what happened. The first year was particularly difficult and draining and futile. The second year was . . . better.

Mercifully, most of the details of what happened those two years became lost in the confusion of fear and the distractions of my noisy mind. What remains are jumbled memories of failed lessons, unruly students, and weak attempts to balance my vision of what a student-centered classroom should be with my total inability to establish any center at all—personal or professional. What I do remember vividly, though, is that after two years in that school, I was miraculously accepted into a Masters program in literature; turned down a contract offered for a third year of teaching; resigned my position; and retreated to the university, where I drove a bus to make money. I was back behind the wheel. At that point my failure might have been complete and the teaching part of my life over except for the lingering results of my previous actions and their effects on my own noisy and persistent mind: taking a teaching job and then leaving it without ever feeling I had mastered it created serious questions for me that followed me into graduate school and dogged me for years. What had happened to me? What did those two years out of my life mean? Why, really, had I failed? What was it I needed to know that I hadn't known? How could I find it out?

What You Sow, So Shall You Reap

All our actions have results, if not today then tomorrow—or ten years from tomorrow. This is the law of karma, and there is no escaping it. For me, karma extended all the way to the unanswered questions about my short teaching life that I tried to leave behind when I quit my job, finished the M.A. program, and began to climb what people used to call a "career ladder." Graduate school had taught me to be a good student finally, and since I had secondary school teaching experience I went directly into a Ph.D. program in . . . what else? English education! When I finished that degree program I got a good job teaching beginning English teachers at a small university, where I was quite happy. Not content, apparently, to be "quite happy," I climbed on after seven years to what seemed at the time to be a "better job." After ten more years of various pleasant and unpleasant experiences, I am now perched on some rung of my career ladder and look to be, from one point of view at least, the main character in a very modest success story: truck driver becomes teacher, becomes graduate student, becomes bus driver, gets Ph.D., gets good job, gets tenure, gives up tenure to get another job, gets tenure again, becomes administrator, etc.

But that is a limited way of looking at it, which overlooks the effects of the questions I left unanswered at the bottom of the ladder. Questions like that do not go away. How stupid of me to think that I could improve my perch and succeed as a teacher educator while leaving my failure as a teacher virtually unexamined. And sure enough, before I knew it I was failing again, this time as a teacher educator, and even while I tried to believe otherwise, the day was coming when I would have no choice but to face the truth.

The Day That Came

Once, I had a student teacher who was a very good student, a very good teacher, and an all-around good person. Years before she became my student she had given me a bird dog, which was a very good bird dog indeed. Everything was good. So naturally, when she finished her student teaching and what seemed to be a good job for her opened up, I made a couple phone calls on her behalf. One of the people I called was the chair of the English department in a high school in the city where I worked. This department chair had also been my student once and was one of the finest teachers I have ever known. In addition, I had worked with her on many projects and had supervised a good number of student teachers in her department over the years. The day I called her about my student I felt like a rip-roaring success who had good connections with good people.

Apparently the department chair did not see it the same way. At first when we were on the phone together and I was speaking with her about my student—as I had spoken with other people about other students in the past—she seemed to be listening to me and even agreeing with what I was saying. All of a sudden, though, something happened that completely shattered the pleasant delusion that I had been manufacturing for several years across many rungs of the ladder. All of a sudden, seemingly out of nowhere, she ripped into me the way a bush hog rips through undergrowth. The heart of what she had to say was this: "Bob Tremmel, you don't know shit about teaching, you don't know shit about high schools, and you're a complete idiot and failure." Even though to this day I cannot say for sure exactly what she was referring to, I believed her. I absolutely believed her.

Such moments have the potential to be defining moments in any person's life. I still remember standing there in the kitchen of my house with the phone in my hand. I still remember looking out the window to where a piggish male grackle was squatted down in the bird feeder staring at me with a fierce gold-and-black eye. I do not remember anything else or exactly what happened after that. Perhaps the bird flew away. But I do remember the sick feeling that spread through me the rest of that morning into the afternoon, which I carried with me all summer, and which escorted me into the new school year, the fall, and the winter. Even though my student got the job and I occasionally saw the department chair after that, I never said anything to her again— not out of anger, but out of a profound sense of failure and embarrassment—and the following spring I took another job and left that city for good.

Someone Else's Day

In my new job, which was exactly like my old one only much more difficult and stressful, I was lost. Even though I managed to function in a way that was at least acceptable to most others, any sense I had ever had that I knew what I was doing was gone. It became clearer and clearer to me that even though my courses usually ran well and my students taught well and often got jobs, whatever it was I had not known in my first teaching job I still did not know.

To some, these suspicions of mine might seem like paranoid delusions or an overreaction to criticism. However, a few years ago I read an article in *English Journal* by Sally Hudson-Ross and Patti McWhorter which suggested to me that ignorance, failure, and a nagging sense of something missing are not uncommon among teacher educators. Like me, Hudson-Ross is an English education professor at a large university. Also like me, she found that lingering questions about her teaching ability pursued her from the time she left the secondary school classroom and moved into an academic career. In the early 1990s, Hudson-Ross reached a point where she began to feel so uneasy that she no longer had confidence in what she was doing in her work with beginning teachers. When her students would ask her specific questions about how to operate in the schools—questions like "What do I do if a fight breaks out?" or "What do I do if I fail?"—Hudson-Ross became embarrassed with her "simple" answers that passed the buck from her to practicing teachers:

> "You'll learn all that from your cooperating teacher" [Hudson-Ross told her students], "Planning can alleviate most management problems," "You'll learn content as you teach it," "If you are grounded in strong theory, the answers will come," "Don't worry; you'll be fine. . . ."
> (1995, 46)

Finally, Hudson-Ross's doubt crystallized in the awareness that she and the university itself were out of touch with the reality in the schools and that her vague answers to her students were signs that she really did not know what she was talking about. Her reaction to this realization was a bold one: Hudson-Ross traded places with a high school teacher and went back to the secondary school while her counterpart taught at the university. What followed from that was a difficult year in which Hudson-Ross reentered the classroom and experienced the shock of her failure to function there, the shock of finding out that her life was not at all what she had thought it was, and finally, thankfully, the shock of realizing that at the heart of failure lie the seeds of understanding.

Hudson-Ross learned in the end that her failure and what was missing for her did not have much to do with the kinds of things that usually occupy educational researchers, scholars, and teacher educators. Professionally, she was doing everything right: planning every detail in every day, teaching her students everything she was supposed to teach them, working as hard as she could. Working too hard: she was trying to do everything for all her students herself, getting up at 5:00 A.M., staying at school until 6:00 or 7:00 P.M., and working until bedtime. In the end, what turned out to be missing was much more important than teaching. What turned out to be missing was living, learning to live the life of a teacher—which means first of all learning to live the life that is the life of yourself. Here is a passage from Hudson-Ross's article in which she shares with other teachers—both beginning and experienced—a very simple but important bit of professional knowledge that almost never finds its way onto the methods class syllabus:

> "Let it go. Give it up. Lighten up." became my mantra. I let myself go to the grocery store again with my husband. I forced myself to stay in bed until 6 a.m., even if I was awake and thinking earlier. I left school with the others, and learned to work pleasurably on school matters at a local fast-food restaurant for an hour or two instead (with free Diet Coke refills). At home, I only worked on weekends. I asked my husband about his work, and took up golf again. I saved time for friends, movies, and laughter. In short, I regained my self. . . . In teaching, and perhaps in life, real control means having the courage to let go of the debilitating, overpowering, All-American need to do better and to do

more in order to succeed. The control I had needed all along was not over kids, the curriculum, or my vision, but over myself so that kids could be free to learn. (1995, 50)

Very surprising indeed. In the end, her sense of failure led Hudson-Ross to understand that what is important is not just academic knowledge about how to function in the classroom, but also personal knowledge about who the teacher is, how to understand oneself as a teacher and human being, and how to live the life of a teacher in school and out of school. Who would have figured that as significant as rhetorical theory, literary criticism, and lesson planning truly are, an equally significant area of study might be grocery shopping?

One Night

Yes, who would have figured it? But this, basically, is what I ended up learning about my failures as a teacher and teacher educator too. Too many of the questions I could not answer were the wrong questions, and the moves I tried to make in order to succeed were the wrong moves. Like Hudson-Ross, I was looking for the wrong things in the wrong places. Unlike Hudson-Ross, though, I did not find what I needed in the grocery store. For me, years of failure and doubt coalesced one night in the middle of a snowstorm around a question one of my students asked me.

Each week toward the beginning of the student-teaching term, I meet with my student teachers in an informal gathering that is part seminar, part group therapy session, and part party. Sometimes we meet in a classroom on campus, a school within easy distance of where most of the students are teaching, at a restaurant, or at someone's house. One particular week near the start of the spring term, I was sitting with a half dozen students in an apartment. Outside, wet, heavy snow driven by an east wind was falling, and I remember being very uneasy, not only as a physical reaction to the low pressure of the weather system, but also by the prospect of having to drive thirty miles home after our meeting. I remember wishing we could just finish and leave, but the student teachers kept talking and talking and asking and asking questions.

I remember, the light was low in the apartment, and I was sitting on a straight chair. My students were scattered around on various kinds of furniture and on the floor. In that group there was a student named Rachel who, in all the years I have been in this business, was the best student I have ever had. I remember, out of nowhere she asked me a question. I do not remember exactly how she put the question to me, but I do remember the general shape and lineaments of it, and as she spoke I remember how a jolt of recognition flashed through my mind and body and suddenly I experienced the kind of "Aha" that Hudson-Ross may have experienced in the produce aisle reaching for the portobello mushrooms. For the very first time I was able to see the faint outline of answers to the questions I had been struggling with since leaving my first teaching job with my tail tucked between my legs and my nose headed upwind.

Rachel, who was struggling herself for the first time with the difficulties of teaching practice that had defeated me, asked a question about how long it should take to return her students' writing to them after they handed it in to her. As sincere and meaningful as that question was, it was, like the questions I had always asked, the wrong question. The right question, what she really wanted to know but didn't yet know how to ask, was, "How is it possible to do this hard, sometimes impossible work day after day, year after year, do it well, and still maintain a reasonable quality in my private and professional life?"

This really is the question, is it not? Although she really did want to know about returning student work, Rachel was not just asking me what to do or how to do it. She was also asking me—of all people—how to practice, how to work, how to live, how to live with her work. Even though I know I had encountered it many times before, up until that moment I had never really heard this question-within-an-infinite number-of-questions, understood it, or considered it for myself. Up until that moment, like Hudson-Ross, I had never been able to see the basic truth: none of the questions we ask as teachers or teacher educators are the right questions until we can understand them in two ways—first, in the specific contexts bound by the details of daily practice; and second, simultaneously, in the much larger context that reaches all the way down and all the way out and takes in not only the lives we live in the school, but our whole lives. Questions about teaching must be more than questions about teaching; they must be questions about living, too.

Days of Pain

It is legitimate to ask why, after being in the dark for so long, Rachel's question made me see my life differently, and why, in the instant she spoke, the narrow world I had been living in became a much larger world, with my professional life expanding suddenly into my life as a whole. The reason, I think, was that in order for me to be even ready to hear what she was saying, I first needed to learn another lesson that I had been working on during all the years of my failure. Even though it might seem like a bit óf a digression, I want to talk for just a little bit about pain.

Almost from the time I first decided to become a teacher I had been in pain. It started innocently enough: simple ailments here and there, sleeplessness, tiredness. By the time I was into my early years of graduate study, though, the simple ailments intensified and stretched themselves out. I started having trouble with chronic infections that seemed to come and go without cause or reason. Medication worked idiosyncratically or not at all. Unaccountably I would get sick, then well, then immediately sick again. My doctors were amazed, annoyed, angry, and sympathetic all at once. I was in pain and had no idea why.

Then, in the summer of 1978, when I was about to start a new teaching job within my graduate program, these small failures of the body turned downright nasty. Most of the preceding year I had been running, not just jogging, increasing my distance, pushing myself toward some as yet unstated goal. I felt better than I had in years. Running was my salvation. It made me feel good, made the stress I was feeling in my life bearable, and seemed to reduce, if not eliminate, the pain. It was so easy: all I had to do was step out my front door and miles later I would feel cleansed, relaxed, and content. Running balanced me, and I was convinced that as long as I had running in my life I would be fine and nothing that had ever bothered me in the past would ever bother me again.

That summer the pain started in my left ankle and heel and spread up the Achilles tendon in one direction and across the *plantar fascia* in the other direction. At first I ignored the pain and kept running, but it got worse. Then I decided I would just run through it, but it got even worse. At that point I started reading books and articles about running. I bought ankle supports, over-the-counter pain medications, and various snake oil remedies in tubes, jars, and squeeze bottles. But the pain got worse. And the swelling. And then I came to a stop.

The clinic at the university hospital where I ended up had, people said, some of the best orthopedists in the world, but nothing they did helped me. Cortisone did not help. Ultrasound did not help. Week after week I hobbled back into the clinic and the doctors rubbed their chins in frustration. Finally, one of them lost his patience and slapped a cast on me. That is when my problems really started. I carried that cast, without a walking device, on my left leg for a month. By the time it came off my already weakened leg and foot had atrophied to the point where I thought I could see bone through the smooth, flaccid skin. Pain was flowering all over my body from the crippling effects of living on one foot. Just getting to a class, never mind teaching it, was an ordeal. For that entire fall, winter, and following spring I lived with crutches, a cane, braces, pain.

It was a long time before I started to get better, years long, years of physical therapy, acupuncture, and various hard lessons about the complex and unpredictable relationships that can develop between body and mind. At some point in this process, I am not sure exactly when, I showed up at the office of a biofeedback therapist. Biofeedback is an excellent way to deal with pain. It is based on a repertoire of techniques that helps one to become aware of the state of body and mind and to control basic mental and physical processes, including pain. The first biofeedback technique I learned, for example, was to control the temperature of my hands and feet. In order to do this I went into my bedroom, sat quietly in a chair, and hooked myself up to a specially made thermometer. Then I either concentrated directly on the body part I wanted to warm up or repeated over and over to myself a series of phrases like, "My finger is getting warm. My hand is getting warm. My arm is getting warm." Strange and improbable as it seemed to me at first, such methods were not only successful at raising the temperature of my appendages, but succeeded in reducing my pain as well. But there was an additional effect that I now think of as a gift of the pain. During the biofeedback sessions, alone in my bedroom, for the first time in my life, I became aware of my thoughts.

I do not mean that up until that point in my life I had no awareness at all of my thoughts. What I mean is that it was not until I practiced the discipline of biofeedback, by sitting without distraction in a quiet room and trying to focus my mind, that I discovered my thoughts were so pervasive and persistent—and so noisy—that my mind was not close to being focused. Initially, I was shocked to discover what was going on in my mind, and I was even more shocked in the days that followed my initial discovery to learn that it went on all the time: words; images; dreams; fantasies; delusions; worries; long, involved planning sessions devoted to the most trivial aspects of my life. No wonder I was in pain. I was beating myself mercilessly with an around-the-clock, out-of-control barrage of thinking that my body could not help but respond to—unfortunately, often in the most negative ways.

The next time I went to see the biofeedback therapist I asked him about this. Without saying much he handed me a book titled *Zen Mind, Beginner's Mind* by a Zen Master in San Francisco named Shunryu Suzuki. In that book one of the things that Suzuki writes about is zazen, the basic practice of Zen meditation, which involves just silent and immobile sitting in an upright, cross-legged posture. I tried it, and the first thing I discovered was that it was a great deal like biofeedback only much more uncomfortable. I sat and watched my mind race. I tried following Suzuki's instructions for breathing: "When we practice zazen our mind always follows our breathing" (1970, 29). I followed my breathing, in and out. The quality and volume of my mind activity immediately changed and I became quieter, more focused. But then, just as immediately, I lost contact with my breath, my mind wandered, and the volume went up. I came back to breathing: in and out. Up and down. My mind wandered again. And again. I returned. Wandering and returning. Breathing in and out. I kept breathing in and out.

Still Breathing Each Day

By the time Rachel asked her question I had been breathing in and out, practicing Zen for about seven years. I started alone, at first sitting sporadically, then daily, and later with various teachers, all of whom had either direct contact with Shunryu Suzuki or with students or associates of his. During those years I had ample time to study my pain and to see that just as my mind was always busy and thoughts continually came up and passed away, so was my body always busy, reacting to everything in my environment from my thoughts to the food I ate, and that pain, along with a multitude of other sensations, continually arose and passed away. The kind of pain I had (I cannot speak for other people's pain), I discovered, was not some abnormal event that occurred in an isolated section or mechanism of my body. Rather, it existed as a part of my whole body, my whole life, as naturally as my breath.

I truly believe that if I had not had this experience with pain and had not learned what I did, I would never have been able to understand what Rachel was really asking me. When she spoke, I suddenly saw that the same thing I had learned about the difficulties of pain had to be true of returning student writing or any other difficult aspect of the teacher's life. Trying to make sense of questions about teaching without looking at them in the context of the teacher's whole life suddenly seemed as futile to me as trying to cure a pain in my foot by treating it as if it were separate from my whole body and mind, the whole life I was living. Pain, a potent and patient teacher, had finally taught me something about connections, and when I connected with Rachel's question I was ready for it in a way I could not have been otherwise.

That does not mean, however, that I was ready for the answer I gave her, which came out of my mouth completely unplanned and unpremeditated, and which surprised me as much as it must have her. Despite its quirky quality, though, I understood in that moment that what I was trying to communicate was nothing less than the fundamental principle upon which a teacher's life and practice rest and that I had been looking for through all the years of failure and pain. I said to her, borrowing the words of another,

Each day is a journey and the journey itself, home.

Even more amazing to me was that this fundamental principle was followed immediately by more unexpected words that spelled out what I have come to think of—with an adequate amount of seriousness—as The Four Pillars of Teaching Practice. They are:

1. Survive.
2. Pay Attention.
3. Begin the Journey.
4. Stay on the Journey.

In the next chapter and the four following it, I will take up in order the Fundamental Principle and the Four Pillars. As I do, I will try to explain what I mean by each of these ideas and why I have come to believe that they are central to living the life of the teacher.

I wish I could say that I was able to produce some kind of coherent explanation the night these ideas first arose, but I have no idea at all how I tried to show my students that I had done anything more than answer a good question with an impenetrable prophetic utterance. Whatever it was I came up with, though, I hope I was able to assure them of my complete sincerity, because I was sincere. The clarity and force with which these ideas occurred convinced me immediately that somehow they had the power not only to help my students, but to help me as well. To me they felt like healing words that, if I could follow them far enough, could show me a way to understand the pain of failure I had carried around for all my years as a teacher; to fill the gaps in my knowledge created by the uneven fit of all the theories, beliefs, opinions, methodologies, and other bits of information that were part of my education; and, finally, to live my life as a teacher.

Chapter Two

The Fundamental Principle

"You are a clever man, Odysseus of Ithaca, but not a very wise one. You keep your eyes only on your home. Blinded, you do not see that it is the journey itself which makes up your life. Only when you understand this will you understand the meaning of wisdom."

—*The Odyssey* (Hallmark
Video Adaptation)

From the very beginning I have thought of the Fundamental Principle and the Four Pillars of Teaching Practice as so basic and foundational that they apply to all curriculums and teaching approaches. I realize that postmodern thinkers who take an antifoundational stance and avoid allegiance to anything that might even resemble a universal principle on which monolithic curricular systems or educational movements could be constructed might find this a disagreeable position. Even though this could bother me, what I am really trying to get at may not turn out after all to be such a contradiction with that point of view. It seems to me that the Fundamental Principle and Four Pillars are so universal and foundational that they are ultimately antifoundational: no creed or school of thought can claim them, and surely no single movement could be built on them. They belong to everyone and to no one. They are to teaching practice what ground is to walking and air is to breathing. Regardless of what theory or viewpoint—foundational or otherwise—dominates a teacher's practice, to live as a teacher means somehow to develop a working sense of the Fundamental Principle and the Four Pillars. There is no escaping it. Surviving, for example, is not an option. Neither is paying attention. Even when I was at the low point in my failings as a teacher somehow I knew that I had to try to keep moving and to figure out what was happening to me. No matter how mindless I might have been I still remember the color of the grackle's eye outside my window while I stood there on the phone, shocked, embarrassed, and ready to run away. Even then I had an idea that paying attention was crucial, though I did not know much about how to do it.

The fact that the Fundamental Principle and the Four Pillars might be tangled up in a postmodern contradiction does not bother me for another reason: I am in good company. Right now our whole discipline is caught in a truckload of contradictions. Recently, two researchers, Peter Smagorinsky and Melissa Whiting, conducted a survey of methods courses in order to try to find out what really goes on in English education programs around the country—to find out who we are, so to speak. What they found out was that there is a surprisingly wide array of theories and approaches that make up the discipline we call English education. An interesting feature of these theories and approaches is that they contradict each other all over the place without those contradictions seeming to do much damage. See for yourself. Here is a sampling of "approaches" they identify (Smagorinsky and Whiting 1995). Perhaps you will recognize a methods course you have taken in here somewhere:

1. *The Survey Approach.* This approach gathers together a wide range of topics and distributes them to education students so they get at least a little bit of everything: grammar, computers, writing, testing and evaluation, debate, discipline, classroom management, and so on (9). These survey courses, Smagorinsky and Whiting say, are designed to "cover all the bases" (10) and tend to include a large number of "brief assignments." In the seventy-nine syllabi from around the country that they studied, the survey approach was the most prominent.

2. *The Workshop Approach.* This approach was the second most prominent, being favored in twenty-three courses compared to twenty-seven for the survey approach. The workshop approach features "students' participation in the activities they are being taught to teach" (12) and moves from theory to practice in an integrated fashion. In workshops the work focuses on student writing, response, reading journals, and extended process-oriented activities.

3. *The Experience-based Approach.* This approach "deliberately links theory and practice" through extensive field experiences punctuated

with class sessions, discussions, readings, and other more typical academic work. In terms of relative prominence there was a large drop-off after the "survey" and the "workshop" approaches, with the experience-based approach represented by only eight out of the total seventy-nine syllabi.

4. *The Theoretical Approach.* This approach, represented in four of the seventy-nine syllabi, favors, as one might expect, theory over practice. Courses based on this approach appear to assume that an understanding of theoretical underpinnings will inform practice.

5. *Reflective Approaches.* These various approaches, which were lightly represented in the study, were based on students' developing an ability to observe themselves and others operating in a variety of in-class and out-of-class situations. The idea behind reflective approaches is that such practices will help teachers learn to think for themselves. Typical activities in classes based on reflective approaches might involve practical experience as well as journals, portfolios, and other forms of writing that are commonly understood to be "reflective."

And here is a sampling of "theories and issues" that underlie English education programs:

1. *Developmental.* This is a theoretical framework based on the work of Piaget and on the assumption that language teaching should follow the natural contours of the way human beings grow and develop. This theory represents a naturalistic view toward student growth and leads toward teaching that is, according to Smagorinsky and Whiting, "synonymously labelled student centered, holistic, whole language, experience centered, or personal growth" (55).

2. *Transactional.* This theory is most closely associated with reader response theories of criticism, particularly the work of Louise Rosenblatt. According to Smagorinsky and Whiting the transactional view "explicitly challenges the dichotomy between mind and matter typified by Piagetian approaches to learning" (64) and focuses on the constructive nature of reading in terms of readers' responses to texts in experiential, social, and cultural contexts.

3. *Scaffolding.* The theorists upon whose work Smagorinsky and Whiting base this category represent a wide and varied group that shares a commitment to a more teacher-centered, structured design of activities that involves a large amount of teacher direction at the outset, but which "diminishes as [teacher education] students begin to demonstrate that they have internalized the principles of instruction" (73).

4. *Process.* This theoretical framework is based on the familiar idea that students learn to use language best by doing just that—using language—and that a deductive, piecemeal approach to grammar and correctness inhibits student development.

5. *Sociocultural.* This theory is most closely connected with what we might call "cultural studies" or "social construction." It proceeds from the assumption that schools and other social institutions are structured "according to the patterns of thought and interaction of the white middle class and that persistent patterns of failure, inappropriate behavior, and other presumed 'deficits' of cultural minorities are attributable to differences between learned ways of thinking, knowing, and interacting rather than to cognitive failure" (79). Those working out of this theoretical framework attempt to "liberate" what they see as oppressed or misguided education students and open their eyes to the fundamental inequities in society and to possibilities for social and political action and empowerment.

Make no mistake about it: these approaches and theories contradict each other in fundamental, even foundational, ways. For example, since social constructionists are focused on understanding individuals in social and cultural contexts, they do not look with favor on theories and approaches like "developmental" and "scaffolding" that seem, on the surface anyway, to consider individuals as apolitical—even isolated—entities. Likewise, those favoring so-called naturalistic developmental approaches feel uncomfortable with scaffolders and social constructionists, whom they see as overly teacher-centered, directive, or even authoritarian in the pursuit of their own agendas.

In trying to make sense of these contradictions and figure out what it is English educators actually do, Smagorinsky and Whiting demonstrate that our discipline has somehow developed the ability to contain many contradictory viewpoints at the same time and still maintain its professional integrity. This should please the antifoundationalists since it shows that there is not even a hint of a single, universal movement that threatens to take all of us over. This should likewise please those with foundational yearnings, since it gives them a generous and free supply of conceptual frameworks with which to associate themselves. In fact, Smagorinsky and Whiting themselves at one point declare that "all [English educators] strive for learning that is constructive, student-centered, empowering, and meaningful" (92), which is a foundational principle if I have ever heard one.

Smagorinsky and Whiting's broad and open view of English education helps me feel comfortable with the contradiction that seems to lie at the center of this book and, inescapably, at the center of my teaching life. All of us need to feel comfortable with contradiction.

Contradiction is built into the basic fabric of our discipline, whether it involves moving among contradictory paradigms or whether it involves maintaining contradictory views simultaneously. Surely there must be at least some room here for an unassuming Fundamental Principle and a few Pillars. This seems especially true when you consider that their point of origin lies in a region of thought that some people would say represents the heartland of contradiction itself.

Basho

The source for the line that makes up the fundamental principle for teaching is the very first entry of *Oku-No-Hosomichi*, a travel journal written by the seventeenth-century Japanese Zen Haiku poet Basho. To call *Oku-No-Hosomichi* just a travel journal, though, is a bit like calling *Paradise Lost* just a religious poem. The short entries in it, while they do describe the daily progress of Basho and his disciple, Sora, on a long pilgrimage in the north of Japan, do a great deal more, concerning themselves deeply with spiritual matters and frequently breaking into poetry. According to D. T. Suzuki (not to be confused with Shunryu Suzuki, the Zen Master I introduced in Chapter 1), a leading twentieth-century Zen scholar and practitioner, Basho was the poet most responsible for raising the haiku from "mere wordplay without contact with life" (1970, 257) to a form that is able to apprehend and give shape to experience and perceptions of reality.

Despite the fact that the words and the life of someone like Basho might seem far removed from the work of a present-day teacher, this is not the case. But in order to understand the connection it is first necessary to see how short, cryptic forms like the ones Basho thought and wrote in function to represent understanding and feeling. One way to get an idea about this is to turn to the work of a contemporary poet named Jack Collom who has extensive experience teaching poetry writing to students in schools. Collom helps his students see how just a few words can say a great deal by teaching them to write "lunes," a short haiku-like poetic form. The formal Japanese haiku, as it is commonly understood in this country, is a three-line poem with a syllabic pattern of 5-7-5 syllables per line. The lune, Collom says, "is a simplification of formal haiku" in which the students count words instead of lines so they do not become "overly concerned with the mere mechanics" (1985, 3). For example, one of Collom's students, a fifth grader in Nebraska, wrote the following lune:

> When the sun's
> rays hit the shades, it
> lights up lines. (3)

Even though this poem may seem very simple on first glance, it does
not take very much reflection to see there is a great deal going on in it.
Collom explains:

> It is also a deceptively complex maze of sound correspondences and
> play: simple rhythms in lines one and three contrasting with syn-
> copation of line two (differing syllable lengths, comma pause, conso-
> nantal percussion), n's around soft "the" in line 1 forming a sound-
> swing, "rays-shades" assonance and "hit-it" rhyme, soft central "the"
> repeated, five terminal s's, "lights-lines," "suns-up," n again in "lines,"
> t in "lights"—until "lights up lines" carries more import than the
> physical window pattern alone. The lines of the poem are lit up too. I
> advise students that the author probably didn't calculate all this but
> that a careful, though non-specific, concentration can let the musical
> phrases come. . . . Sometimes I tell [students] lunes are like looking
> through a crack; even the plainest sight may look interesting, due to
> the focus. (3–4)

The key to understanding what is happening in the lines of a lune
or a haiku or a Zen travel journal—or life itself, perhaps—is to do
what Collom advises: look very closely and be ready to find more than
seems obvious at first. Before using Collom's way of reading to explain
the Fundamental Principle, I want to show further how his approach
works by applying it to one of Basho's own short poems. In entry 41 of
Oku-No-Hosomichi, Basho writes of coming to an inn where he over-
hears two prostitutes talking in the next room. Like Basho and Sora
these prostitutes are also on a pilgrimage, and that night in the inn they
are bemoaning their miseries and lot in life. Basho writes this haiku:

> in the same house
> girls of pleasure also slept
> hagi and moonlight

Even though there is no way I can begin to unpack this whole poem
here, I do think I can show line by line how it participates, like the fifth
grader's lune, in a surprisingly deep and broad rendering of experience.
Hopefully, understanding how this piece works will provide insight into
how to go about interpreting the Fundamental Principle.

"In this house"

This poem depicts a remarkable, but probably not uncommon, coming
together under one roof of serious spiritual practitioners with people
not usually considered under the heading of "spiritual." The situation
is even more remarkable—even paradoxical—because all the travelers
are on pilgrimage. In this line there is no sense of disapproval in the
poet's tone, nor is there in the larger journal entry, of which the poem

is a part. On the contrary, the poet accepts and respects the women just as they are, though he is unable to help relieve their unhappiness. When they ask Basho if they might follow along behind him on their way he gently informs them that

> "Unfortunately [Sora and I] often like to take detours. Just follow anyone going your way. Surely the gods will protect you and see you safely through." Words lift them on leaving, but felt sorry for them for sometime after. (n.p.)

Basho is a kind man who offers a kindly solution to the women's problem, but he also firmly refuses to be guide or teacher. Ironically, though, embedded in his refusal to teach is a potent bit of teaching. "Look for the solution to your problems in someone going your way, not someone going my way," Basho seems to say, indicating the need for student and teacher to be of like mind, like spirit, and headed in the same direction. Standing behind this teaching is a central term in Basho's thinking: "way." "Way" is not just the *way* (as in direction) one is traveling or the *way* (as in method) one makes the journey, but also the "Way": the "Way" of life, the "Spiritual Way," or even the "Way" of haiku poets. Dogen, a Zen teacher who lived four hundred years before Basho, connected "Way" with the teachings of Buddha and wrote of it this way:

> Students should know that the . . . Way lies outside thinking, analysis, introspection, knowledge, and wise explanation. If the . . . Way were in these activities, why would you not have realized the . . . Way by now, since from birth you have perpetually been in the midst of these activities?
> Students of the Way should not employ thinking, analysis, or any such thing. Though thinking and other activities perpetually beset you, if you examine them as you go, your clarity will be like a mirror. The way to enter the gate is mastered only by a teacher who has attained [the truth]. (1985a, 39)

This view of the Way as nonconceptual suggests a similar dimension in the Way of every teacher. Teachers are not simply mechanics who apply skills and tools to students by means of intellectual processes. Teachers also rely on their feelings, their intuitions, their direct perceptions of their students. Basho is not arguing a position or defending a thesis in entry 41, although he could have chosen to do that and achieved his objective just the same. What he is doing is expressing by other means what he knows by other means: he is not the right one for the women. Instead of becoming their teacher, he teaches them how to find their teacher by looking for someone who is going their own Way.

Another way of putting it is to say that Basho teaches out of his gut as much as out of his head. It must be the same for all teachers. Head without gut will not take a teacher too far. Neither will gut without head. A teacher can only go the whole Way with the whole body and mind.

John Dewey, who was certainly very skilled at rational thought, made a point similar to Dogen and Basho when he said that teaching is not a science that we can analyze, formulate, and break down into parts. Rather, it is an art in which the artists may intellectually know what they are doing, but must operate also to a large degree on the basis of their personal knowledge and feeling sense of their art. Gut and mind. Mind and gut.

"Girls of pleasure also slept"

Basho and Sora sleep in the house and presumably others also sleep "in the same house." But there is a much richer undercurrent running through this line. What is it the women do besides "also" sleep? We know from the entry as a whole that Basho and Sora hear them talking. What else? How do the women interact with the others in the house? What do all those who stop together for the night share? What is brought together here in what Ways? What actions, what effects of karma led all the pilgrims to this house? What led Basho and Sora to a place where prostitutes "also" sleep? What led the women to a place where a Zen poet and teacher "also" sleeps? What storm blew them all together?

This line leaves us with many more questions than it answers. Other than to make it clear that he refuses to make judgments, Basho is no more eager to offer answers here than he is to guide and answer the questions of the women. One of the reasons for this is that he knows very well he does not have the answers. This is a very important point for all teachers to consider. Most educational systems in most countries are based on the premise that teachers know what there is to be known and that they have the answers to all the important questions. In fact, teachers have pieces of paper that testify to this knowledge. Some teachers actually believe strongly in their pieces of paper, are very proud of what they know, and get disturbed when their knowledge, beliefs, and opinions are called into question by other people—especially students or their parents. All of us are probably like this to varying degrees, and when our attachment to ourselves-as-experts is very strong it can prove to be a great hindrance to both teaching and learning. All of us, I believe, would benefit from a measure of Basho's humility and reserve. Sometimes we know just what to do and how to do it. Sometimes we just do not know the Way and there is little to say about it.

Paulo Freire, a contemporary Brazilian teacher and scholar, discussed this need for humility on the part of teachers in the context of what he called a "critical" or "liberating" view of education. Liberating teachers do not set themselves apart or above their students. Instead, they enter into the transaction of learning with them by listening and receiving knowledge as well as speaking and sharing their own knowledge. Liberating teachers, Freire says, do not talk *to* their students, but talk *with* them and learn with them. Freire has a very low opinion of proud, know-it-all, "authoritarian" teachers:

> Only authoritarian educators deny the solidarity between the act of educating and the act of being educated by those becoming educated; only authoritarians separate the act of teaching from that of learning in such a way that he who believes himself to know actually teaches, and who is believed to know nothing learns. In truth, . . . it is necessary for the one who knows to understand that no one knows everything and that no one is ignorant of everything. (1992, 41)

Let me cite another contemporary example of what I am getting at here. George Kalamaras, a college writing teacher, once worked as a writing-across-the-curriculum consultant to a university biology department. It was Kalamaras's job to help the teaching assistants who were assigned to teach the biology writing component. The big problem with this was that those teaching assistants did not really want his help, did not want to teach writing, and really did not want to have anything at all to do with consultant Kalamaras. (This was a situation not unlike the situations many middle and high school English teachers find themselves in—teaching students who do not want to be taught.) Despite being unwanted and unrespected, Kalamaras went ahead and did what he figured a consultant should do, which was to function as a knowledgeable expert with worthwhile opinions and beliefs whose job was to teach less knowledgeable people what to do and why. Unfortunately for Kalamaras this did not work, and the harder he tried the more hostile the teaching assistants became and the less he accomplished.

One day he entered the biology lab and found the assistants standing around a fish tank full of leeches. They were throwing zebra fish in with the leeches to see how long it would take for the leeches to consume the fish and turn "flesh to bone," as Kalamaras put it. The first fish Kalamaras watched adopted an evasive pattern that quickly turned into a predictable routine that, unfortunately for the fish, the leeches had no problem mastering. A second fish, though, adopted a pattern that was not a pattern. Instead, it swam in completely unpredictable, apparently non-zebra-fish-like directions and so was able to keep flesh and bone together. Seeing this caused Kalamaras to realize that, trapped as he was in his predictable role of knowledgeable consultant, he was being eaten alive by the vicious biology teaching assistants. He realized also that the first step toward surviving his predicament was to abandon what he thought he knew, abandon his beliefs and opinions about himself, abandon his teaching approaches, and swim off in a new and completely unpredictable direction. It was only at that point that he began to get any real consulting and teaching done.

To follow the examples of Freire, Kalamaras, and Basho by giving up strong attachment to what we think we know and our need to know is not easy, but sometimes it is necessary in order to discover what it is we really must do. It is not so easy to survive in a leech tank if you are a fish with a narrow mind.

"Hagi and moonlight"

Here is where the poet makes his power move. Hagi are bush clover (*lespedeza striata*), a common plant that flowers in the autumn in Japan. In this line the scene in the house is suddenly blended in with the landscape around it, the whole natural world, the earth and beyond. Here is how D. T. Suzuki comments on this line, which he translates as "the bush clovers and the moon":

> The prostitutes are no more fallen specimens of humanity; they are raised to the transcendentally poetic level with the . . . flowers in their unpretentious beauty while the moon impartially illuminates good and bad, comely and ugly. There is no conceptualization here, and yet the haiku reveals the mystery of being-becoming. ([1970] 1989, 230)

Suzuki's last point, that "there is no conceptualization here," makes once again a central point that lies behind the method of haiku as well as the Way of teachers. As much as we know and want to know, there is only so much we can understand through conceptual thinking. Just as Kalamaras finally became an effective teacher by essentially abandoning teaching, often we can only think through the questions in life and in teaching practice by not thinking. Basho really does not know what else to say about the prostitutes. So he turns to the "hagi and moonlight" and lets them speak while he remains silent.

Suzuki's point also puts me back in contact with the scene in my student teacher's apartment where we were all "also gathered" and brought together by a broad web and pattern of action. My answer to my student teacher's question slipped out of my mouth instinctively, intuitively, without thinking or conceptualizing—in a way not nearly as profound but not dissimilar either to the way Suzuki understands the third line of the haiku. For me, answering my student's question about living the teacher's life the way I did represented a step into the unknown. If I had been operating in my usual teacherly way—if I had been thinking, in other words—I probably would have adopted that familiar and predictable strategy of giving my students information about methods, workload, and preparation time—all matters they had heard a great deal about and matters I certainly discuss much more frequently than I blurt out lines from seventeenth-century Japanese travel journals. But what happened with me when Basho's words leaped out of my mouth felt very much like the way the surprising turn in the haiku feels: a moment of insight when the laboring mind clears and all at once there is the shock of recognition—and the sense that the boundaries of the world are moving outward and inward at the same time.

And this is what it is like to read Basho: looking deeply at even a few words can open us up to the poet and teach us much more than might at first seem possible. Next I want to follow this same approach and try to explain the Fundamental Principle and what it is I mean when I say that in our profession "each day is a journey and the journey itself, home."

"Each Day"

The idea of "each day" is very simple. Each day is just each day. The morning of each day we rise and begin to do the things we do each day. For a teacher this probably means rising quite early, tending to personal needs, taking care of other members of the family, working the school day, returning home, and taking care of more home business. In addition, many teachers, especially those who are most committed, regularly devote out-of-school time to school work: planning the next day, responding to student writing, reading, studying, or writing. Even though being a teacher means having a very demanding regular schedule to keep, each day is different. Some days when we get up, we do not feel so good. Other days we feel great—like we could go out and beat the world into submission and grind the universe into dust without eating breakfast. Some days things go well—there are no problems. Other days seem unlivable—even before school starts: a child is sick, a spouse is unpleasant, the dog gets in the mud, the car keys mysteriously disappear. Each day is each day.

At school each day is each day too. Mondays, for example, can be difficult for both teachers and students. It sometimes seems as if no one really wants to get back into the rituals and routines that the institution and its systems mechanically repeat each day, day in and day out. Wednesday is hump day. Fridays, everyone may be up, looking ahead to the weekend. Or bone tired. Sometimes teachers will wear special or more casual clothing on Friday—a school sweatshirt or jeans. It is amazing how even a little change in dress can change a day. Also, the

big game may be coming up on Friday night, and everyone may be excited—and distracted. Distraction can make any day easier—or more
difficult.

Each class period during each day is different too. The first couple
periods of the day the students might be sluggish, tired. The teacher
might be also. It could be, too, that the first-period class is made up of
lively students whose energy level runs very close to the red line. That
is unusual, but it happens. Before lunch and after lunch might be a
bit—or a lot—exciting, with low blood sugar making everyone rest-
less leading up to the bell and the frivolity of the lunch period lingering after. Last period of the day students may be anxious to get out the
door. Sometimes the time or day of the week makes no difference. Days
with assemblies and special activities can be positive or challenging or
nearly impossible. The day before the holidays . . . The state wrestling
tournament . . . The last day of school . . . Each day is each day; who
knows what it will bring?

Once I did some work in a small school district close to an urban
center. The community the school was in had many problems. Some of
the people living there did not have much money. There was also a
higher than usual level of violence and drug and alcohol use. This carried over, naturally, to the students in the high school. One morning
when I was there I stood by the front door with a teacher when the
bell rang to admit the students for the day. We counted students who
seemed to us to have been obviously drinking or using drugs—mainly
marijuana—before school. We figured 20 percent. This kind of behavior obviously had a big impact on what happened each hour each day.
The drinkers were loud and boisterous early in the morning. By lunch
time, though, they had quieted considerably and many of them, I am
sure, had the beginnings of hangovers. The dope smokers, on the other
hand, were quiet and easygoing, giggly, distracted, and decidedly unfocused. They were much more interested in keeping to themselves
and eating candy than they were in their studies.

Recently, during a meeting, one of my student teachers, Wally, who
had been teaching only a couple weeks, told a similar story. He was observing a class in his cooperating teacher's room when a student came
in who, in Wally's opinion, had clearly been smoking marijuana. All
the symptoms were there: the eyes, the smell, the characteristic non
sequiturs in speech and behavior. After class Wally told his cooperating teacher, Bob, about his observation. Bob was incredulous, but since
Wally was someone to be believed when it came to the ways of the
street, Bob followed up and had the student sent to the office. In the
office the vice principal was also incredulous—even cynical—about
the student teacher's judgment, as were the clerical workers and everyone else. It is easy to imagine the pressure and the stress Wally felt in

pursuing intervention that no one else supported on behalf of a student no one thought needed help. But after a short examination by the school medical and security people, and a few direct questions to the student from the vice principal, the truth came out and Wally was proven right. How was it no one else in the school was able to see what Wally saw? Why would no one believe him? One of the qualities of each day is that when we have been teaching for a while each day often seems so much like every other day, like the same old routine, that we become numb to it and blinded by our expectations. But each day is each day and not any other. Fresh eyes see more clearly.

How each class period each day goes is governed also by each class group—which is different from each other class group. Each blend of individual students with a teacher creates a unique chemistry that may change as students and teachers change over the period of many weeks and months together. Recently, I worked regularly one whole school year with a group of ninth graders in an urban high school. At the beginning of the year they could have fairly been called the class from hell. Two or three of the students were serious troublemakers—gang members. Other students were uninterested. One student, who had a disability, was hounded mercilessly by classmates. During the course of the year, however, a big change occurred in that class. Even though their teacher had little hope, very slowly she began to turn them, to transform them, to help them transform themselves. Each day, again and again she pulled their distracted focus to what she was doing and saying. Some days she let them be silent and sit quietly for long periods of time. Some days she played music for them, quiet, peaceful music. Some days she played audio tapes of running water. Calming. She also held them accountable. Each day. And when the most serious troublemakers were unable to make the turn she required, she had them removed from class. (One or two people—for better or worse—can have a huge impact on a larger group.)

One day toward the end of the school year I was reading some of my poems to this group of students who had been so difficult only a few months before. My purpose was to prepare them to work on their own writing, their own poems. As I read I noticed they were a good audience: attentive, focused, listening carefully, and asking good questions. Eventually, I read the following poem, which is based on my own high school experience:

What I Remember Most About Her

The way she shined her blonde hair
and then floated it somehow
just above her shoulders . . .
or pulled it up behind her ears,

fastened with a barrette
or tiny slice of ribbon . . .
The navy blue sweater . . .
scented notes
taped over the louvers
inside my locker door . . .
gifts tied up in bright colors,
waiting for me
at school in the morning . . .

The little red car she drove
past my house Sunday afternoons,
horn honking for three
solid blocks, coming and going . . .
how she drove
my mother to drinking
and my father to muttering.

The Chevy we drove together,
straddling the crowns of gravel roads,
disappearing without warning
into a gridwork
of possibilities so glowing
and alive, so rare, so near
at hand we could touch them.

*

In the spring, the corn around us
spiked in wet, black loam.
In summer, eight foot stalks hid us;
we swam toward each other
in dark green light.
In fall the leaves
turned brittle, like wrapping paper,
the wind blew
and I went away,
and then one winter soon after
she died and I never knew.

When I had finished reading, one of the students asked me if the poem
was "true." I said that, as much as a poem could be called "true," this
poem was true.

"How sad," the student replied.

"Well," I said, trying to lighten the atmosphere in the room, which
had darkened considerably, "sorry, how about if I read a poem next
that's a complete lie? It's titled 'Fish Story.'"

The disabled student, who was very literal-minded, but also very
sharp, raised his hand and said seriously, "Sir, I really don't think you
should lie."

I was surprised and did not know what to say. One student sitting near me, who not so long before had participated in mocking her classmate, leaned over and said quietly, "Don't worry. He's OK. He's a little different, but we like him." This was a big change in just a few months. What is most important to keep in mind, though, is that it was based entirely on just a little progress each day, each class period each day.

Even the weather can be an important factor in how each day goes. Warm sunny days in the spring can be tough, with everyone wanting to go outside. On hot days in August everyone struggles to concentrate, to keep from sweating on their books and papers. "Readin', Ritin', and Roastin'" is how one student described the 3 Rs of August in schools without air conditioning. And watch out when the barometric pressure starts to drop out in front of a big weather system—or when an arctic high moves in behind and starts to clear out the storm. All animals, with our numerous blood vessels and body cavities containing liquids and air, are like living barometers and react to changes. Fish bite on the leading edge of a cold front and then are sluggish after it passes through. Dropping pressure may put some especially weather-sensitive students—and teachers—on the edge. When the weather changes, my beaten up knees and ankles hurt, and whatever kind of day I am having gets harder.

A Chinese doctor I once went to explained it to me this way. In traditional Chinese medicine three factors are considered when treating a patient: physical condition, psychological condition, and environmental condition. The physical and, to a certain extent, the psychological are factors that we are usually aware of—even though we are not always as attentive to the points where they intersect as we should be. Environmental factors are harder to understand. Teachers should always be aware of the physical conditions in which their students find themselves—this includes the weather. In teaching, as well as in Chinese medicine, environment matters.

So, "each day" is each day. The best way to approach each day is with a flexible, open mind. Even though there is more I will have to say about this kind of mind later, let me say now that there is much in each day we have control over and much that we cannot control. One fundamental point Basho understood very well that helps illustrate this fact is that nothing in our lives or our worlds is permanent. Even though this is an obvious point, most of us do not live each day as if it were; nor do we like to focus on the full implications of impermanence. From one perspective, it is not exaggerating to say that impermanence is the meaning of life on earth. Everything here that I can see, touch, smell, taste, or hear is impermanent, from the planet itself to the cells that make up my body, which are not the cells that made up my body just days or hours ago. Literally, I am not the same person

I used to be, and neither is anybody else. Those individuals we were had no permanence and the individuals we are right now have no permanence. All we really have is each day, or, more precisely, each moment, because moment by moment our miraculous lives burn themselves out just as the sun burns itself out and some day will go cold. This is a sad, even frightening thought, but it does define a common link all of us have with every other being and entity in the physical universe.

I Read Two Articles in the Newspaper This Morning

One said some scientists
have discovered
what they think might be
the "Holy Grail of Cosmology."

It is gas,
massive wisps of gas,
ripples in time and space,
relics of the Big Bang
which banged us all
into being.

The article also said this,
that at one time
all the matter
in the universe
was compressed
into a dense
sphere
smaller than the period
at the end of this sentence.

Imagine that.

Also,
Phillies 8, Cubs 2. (1993–94, 12)

After I wrote this poem I realized that the baseball score in it not only reflects the way the small details in our lives connect with the universal implications of our lives, but also reflect the way we use distractions to help us avoid huge, frightening realities. Instead of accepting and living out our impermanence we exert considerable effort trying to obscure the fact that we are impermanent. We immerse ourselves in pleasant distractions like baseball, establish schedules, standards, patterns, identities that we can hold on to and feel have some lasting value. We buy certain kinds of clothes and certain kinds of vehicles to help reinforce our sense of permanence. We also develop spiritual practices that are based on some kind of permanence, either an afterlife or numerous reincarnations that establish a sort of permanent impermanence. Even though doing such things is absolutely necessary in order for most of us to function as human beings and professionals, if we get lost in them we begin to believe that in this life we are engaged in a permanent, predictable enterprise and that we are in control. The more we kid ourselves into thinking this way, the harder it is to live each day and the more frustrated and angry we become when our plans are disrupted and evaporate and go rippling away.

Developing a loose, flexible, and open mind means developing a mind that can grasp impermanence and is ready for anything, that knows when it is time to put the hammer down and drive forward, and when to pull back, to adjust, to adapt, to abandon plans. It also means learning to flow with the currents of time and circumstance. It means leaving the problems we inevitably have with students, colleagues, and ourselves at the door when we leave school and go home at the end of each day. When we leave, that day is over. All the moments we had are gone. Even though it is hard, it is important to let go of them and to live each day, each moment, exactly and only as we live it and then let it go.

"Each Day Is a Journey"

The journey is a basic motif in the thinking and writing of all cultures and all the world's mythologies, histories, and literatures. Everyone is familiar with Odysseus's ten-year journey to regain his home in Ithaca, Parsifal's search for the Holy Grail, Dante and Christian's epic journeys to achieve salvation. Even though each one of these stories is complex and multilayered, one thing all of them have in common is that they take the form of a quest for some object, place, or state of being. These stories, regardless of their other dimensions, are in that sense highly goal driven and mirror the travels and pilgrimages in both ancient and modern worlds for both secular and spiritual reasons: to Canaan, to Mecca, to Jerusalem, to Fuji, to the North Pole, to the Oregon territory, to the Rose Bowl.

But sometimes journeys do not need to cover all that much ground. One universal way, for example, of understanding the journey is as a purification or preparation for adulthood or other important role in life. Thus, various native cultures send young men out on "Vision Quests" or "Walkabouts" or isolate young women for long periods of time so that they might gain the physical and spiritual power and experience they need to take up full adult roles in the community. At issue in such journeys is not so much where or how far the traveler goes, but the experience of the journey itself.

Such actual and ritual journeys of preparation and purification are at the heart of the legacies of teachers throughout the world and find their significance in day-to-day practice. Jesus journeyed days, not miles, into the wilderness to fast, pray, and prepare to teach. He also journeyed to Jerusalem toward his death and epic days of his passion. Buddha traveled years to get to the Bodhi Tree, where he sat down and resolved not to rise until the morning of the day he achieved enlightenment. That last, immovable journey was his greatest, and only then was he ready to journey back and teach. Indeed, is there any location on earth that is so remote or forbidding that some monk, some missionary, some doctor, some fearless pilgrim will not travel there to get up each day and teach whatever it is that he or she has to teach or to learn what he or she must learn in order to return and teach others? From St. Paul to Jane Goodall, from King Richard to Martin Luther King: these are the journeyers and these are the teachers we model ourselves after, even though their classrooms may have no walls and their students may seek neither diplomas nor degrees—only life.

The journey is important when it comes to understanding not only teaching but ourselves and the world. Human beings are archetypal travelers. The basis for that archetype has probably been integrated in our minds and bodies since the first migrations of Homo Sapiens out of Africa, across Asia, across the Americas, to where the end of the twentieth century finds us poised at the edge of space still trying, day by day, to figure out the way and the Way. Always we are going, going, going: "Two roads diverged in a yellow wood"; "Whan that Aprill with his shoures soote"; "Buck Mulligan came from the stairhead, bearing a bowl of lather on which a mirror and a razor lay crossed." Mountains, deserts, forests, oceans, space, time—each day: all are terrains to be crossed, and when the journey is finally finished the one who completes it, if it has been a sincere pilgrimage and not just a vacation, will not be the one who began it.

The following is a poem I have had in my files for several years. I wrote it when I realized that the time had finally come for me to leave my first university teacher education job and move on to the next. Even though the stink of failure and self pity clings to this poem, there is also—I think—the sense of having completed a journey of sorts—of at least having come to some "place," some "moment," in time—and of having, by virtue of this journey, become someone different than I was when I departed years earlier—and different too than I am now after having journeyed on.

Thanksgiving Prayer

My skin tightens,
then crawls to a complete stop,
mind idling, turning over slowly,
lights dimming into a night

where I can finally see
that even the brightest star
in the sky is rushing
away so fast
there is no hope
of ever catching up.

And I see
at this moment
I am ready,
that all I really
had to do in this life
is done,
that nothing awaits
but more of the same,
that all it has come to
is nothing more
or less,
better or worse,
than this place, this moment,
this sound of wind
blowing through these branches,
and that in the morning,
when the last star
explodes into the distance,
the one who greets its going
will not be the one
who saw it through the night before,
that the words he spoke,
work he did should be left alone,
like so many
feathers after killing,
as if they never were
of any consequence at all,
carried no weight,
created nothing else
to be thankful for,
and no need
to be thankful.

"Each Day Is a Journey
and the Journey Itself, Home"

Even though it is easy to grasp the relationship between the journey
and each day of the journey, Basho's claim that the journey is also
home is not so obvious. One way of getting at it is to begin by thinking

of journeys that are *toward* home or that are a *return* home or that end with the arrival at some new home. Northrup Fry explained this cyclical structure when he described the "heroic quest" in

> the theme of the traditional classical epic where the action begins "in media res," and then works forward to the end and back to the beginning of a cyclical total action. In the *Odyssey*, for example, the total action moves from Ithaca back to Ithaca; in the *Aeneid* from Troy to New Troy, and in *Paradise Lost*, where Christ is the hero, from the presence of God back to his presence again. In each epic the finishing point is the starting point renewed and transformed by the hero's quest. (1963, 262)

Thinking of the journey as abiding in the return moves us a considerable distance away from thinking about the journey as a linear trip from point A to point B. Even "over the river and through the woods to Grandmother's house we go" involves two trips home. A journey really does not need to go anywhere at all or take us somewhere new. Even in a migration, which usually is not the same as a pilgrimage, the purpose is to *re*-turn to a point of origin, to *re*-establish somewhere, to be *re*-born at home.

Truly, wherever our movement leads it is always a movement home. The *Tao Te Ching* is a book of eighty-one short, sometimes mysterious, verses written by the Chinese sage Lao Tsu in the sixth century B.C.E. Verse 40 is one of the shortest and, on the surface at least, one of the most mysterious:

> Returning is the motion of the Tao.
> Yielding is the way of the Tao.
> The ten thousand things are born of being.
> Being is born of not being. (n.p.)

One way of understanding this passage, as well as "the journey itself is home," is to understand first of all the significance of the number 10. Ten is a very big number. There are the "Ten Directions," the "Ten Prohibitory Precepts," the "Ten Commandments," the "Ten Ox-Herding pictures," as well as the "Ten Thousand Things." In learning zazen, Zen meditation, students often learn to take hold of their breathing and their thoughts by counting exhalations through 10 and then returning to 1 and starting the count all over. In addition, students are taught that when (not if!) their minds wander and they find themselves daydreaming, they should—without judging themselves—return to 1 and start all over. In this practice the number 10 becomes the pivot point connected with all returning, the returning motion of meditation, the returning motion of the Tao, the constant returning motion back to 1, back to breathing, the beginning, the here and now, back home.

When you stop and think about it, this counting to the number 10 contains the whole sum of what it means to return. When we start counting we start out with 1, with something, with being. When we reach 10, however, the movement is marked by the addition of a second digit, which is 0, which is nothing, nonbeing. Yet 1 still remains with the 0, and the arrival at nonbeing signals the immediate return to the beginning, to being. Thus, in this continual journey, which is nothing less than our life breath, being cannot be without nonbeing. To say this is "circular" does not even begin to do it justice. In one sense, verse 40 of the *Tao Te Ching*, like Basho's entry 41, like counting to 10, is a highly concentrated distillation of a very far-reaching idea that combines beginning and ending, departure and arrival, into one potent drop. Looked at from this perspective, going and returning, like being and nonbeing, are one, not two, and it is not a very long step from that kind of understanding to the understanding that the journey itself is home.

Even though he would never think along lines like these, I believe my father, who is eighty-five as of this writing, understands what Basho is getting at. Most days when the weather is good my father exercises by walking. He knows perfectly well that the end of his daily journey is not any destination, nor is there any goal of accomplishment as a walker. The end of his journey, like all our journeys, is simply to return home on the way toward a point beyond his ability to move even one millimeter. He walks because it is worthwhile for him to walk and because the journey has value for him. So it is just the journey, the practice itself, he concerns himself with, and the place he arrives each day is the place beneath his feet.

Another way of understanding the interconnectedness of journey, return, home is through Robert Pirsig's *Zen and the Art of Motorcycle Maintenance*. The basic action of this story is based on a journey, a motorcycle trip that the speaker in the book, named Phaedrus after the character in Plato's dialogue, takes with his son, Chris, from Minneapolis to the West Coast. On top of that story Pirsig builds an elaborate construction that contains discussions of philosophy, religion, science, history, motorcycles, and even the teaching of writing. At a point exactly midway through the book Pirsig tells how Phaedrus and Chris go backpacking and climbing for several days in the mountains. Even though Phaedrus, as another character in the book says, is "experienced in the mountains," almost immediately father and son experience problems. Chris finds that backpacking and climbing are not always a great deal of fun. Part of the problem turns out to be that for two weeks just before this trip with his father, Chris had attended a camp where the counselors treated outdoor activities as highly goal-driven tests of manhood. As Phaedrus correctly points out, anyone who treats the mountains as a testing ground for manhood or womanhood is doomed to unhappiness—and perhaps just plain doomed. The mountain never needs to prove its mountainhood to anyone and does not care one little bit about the well-being of others who think they have something to prove.

In this context Pirsig draws a distinction between what he calls the "ego-climber" and the "selfless-climber." The ego-climber is always out of synch and always dissatisfied with where he or she is on the mountain. The focus is on self, on accomplishment, on getting to the top, and since during just about all of a climb the ego-climber is not where he or she wants to be, there is a great deal of unsettledness. The selfless-climber, on the other hand, is focused on the mountain and the action of the moment, has nothing to prove, and consequently has nowhere to go and is settled where he or she is all along the way. There is no conflict between action and goal. All is action, including goal, and the selfless-climber is always present in the present moment of action. Pirsig writes:

> Mountains should be climbed with as little effort as possible and without desire. The reality of your own nature should determine the speed. If you become restless, speed up. If you become winded, slow down. You climb the mountain in an equilibrium between restlessness and exhaustion. Then, when you're no longer thinking ahead, each footstep isn't just a means to an end, but a unique event in itself. . . . To live only for some future goal is shallow. It's the sides of the mountain which sustain life, not the top. Here's where things grow. (1984, 199)

This attitude toward hiking and climbing is pretty close, I think, to Basho's attitude toward the journey. When you are climbing a mountain, that is what you are doing. You are not doing something else or going somewhere else. In a sense, you have nowhere to go. Each step, each breath, each moment totally defines your position, your situation, your being. Mental tuggings of the summit, distractions about speed, goals, and accomplishment take you away from where you are and what you are doing. There is nowhere you must go, because you are there already. Likewise, if we understand each day of our lives as a hike or a climb—or a journey—and if we focus fully on the action at hand, then it is our journey that defines each present moment and is both our destination and our home.

This is not to say, of course, that the goal is to focus so narrowly on the immediate details of the present moment—to get lost in navel gazing—that we totally lose track of the larger context in which we operate. That too is a useless and distracting goal. If the selfless-climber and the day journeyer are not able to support themselves, to plan ahead, to have the right equipment, and so on, then nothing will happen. This is a subtle point, and the way to grasp it is to treat all aspects of whatever practice you are engaged in as action requiring your full attention and care. If your journey of the day takes you on the mountain, you had better plan your route and monitor your progress so you do not get lost or get caught in the open when night or bad weather comes. It would not do to become mesmerized by your bootlaces. Likewise, if your journey for the day is teaching, arranging for your transportation or maintaining a car with which to drive to and from school is an action central to your work. So is planning and studying for advanced degrees; attending conferences; and making sure you have ink in your pen, disks for your computer, and money for retirement.

Even though there is always something up the trail, you cannot live up the trail. But if living where you are does not also include attention to up the trail, then you are lost. Or down the trail: if you cannot apply the lesson you learned yesterday as well as prepare for tomorrow you will lose today. Teaching, like living, is neither one thing nor the other. The one thing leads to all things; all things lead to the one thing. "Each day is a journey and the journey itself, home."

Real Life

In addition to the connections I have made already, this Fundamental Principle taken from Basho applies to teaching in two fundamental ways. First of all, the traveler who is 100 percent traveler and who is totally involved in the journey is a good traveler who knows what is going on. The teacher education student, and then the beginning teacher, and then the experienced teacher who is centered on the practice of teaching and being with students, is a good student and a good teacher who is deeply immersed in the details of the profession. Achieving this kind of focus is especially difficult for students who arrive in my classes at a time when their attention is strongly focused on the future: student teaching, graduating, getting a job, getting married, getting remarried, starting a family, starting a life. Nothing can undo any of us faster than losing focus on the work at hand and getting lost in the future. For a clear mind, for effective teaching, for the journey itself, the point where we find ourselves *right now* must be home.

I remember a student I had once who was trying to student teach while planning a wedding and preparing to move to a place where he and his fiancée could find work and begin their lives together. This student teacher had been an excellent student in classes on campus, but when he went out to student teach he also went over the edge. I remember walking into the classroom where he was teaching American literature one day. He was sitting at a table in front of about twenty-five eleventh-grade students. Several of these students were talking with each other. One was wadding up pieces of paper and throwing them at the wastebasket halfway across the room. Another was standing on a desk, and one boy in the front row was putting his trousers back on. It was an eerie scene, and my student teacher sat in the middle of it just talking about the lesson to himself and to anyone else who would listen. The only clue that he knew something was wrong was that his face was very red and his eyes were bulging so far out of their sockets that I was afraid they would pop loose and roll around like marbles on the floor at his feet. Later, when I talked with him I was able to find out just what a difficult time he was having with so many distractions in his life. From that point on, figuring out how to focus his attention on the work at hand, to *be home* in the classroom even while working for the future, became his practice for the semester. And by the end of the semester he was making solid progress. The key, though, was not simply, as some might have said, for him to learn methods of classroom management. He did need to do this, of course, but the real key was for him to learn self-management, and that meant to find his home in the present moment—and to live there. From that everything else had to proceed.

The second way the Fundamental Principle I draw from Basho applies to teaching has to do with a long-standing confusion we have had in American education. John Dewey addressed this confusion eloquently and often, as have others, but like all deep-seated confusions it stays with us and haunts us. The confusion is the mistaken idea that the purpose of education is to prepare individuals for real life, which is not supposed to begin until schooling ends. This idea exists at all levels, is highly regressive, and imposes limitations that narrow the scope of practice for all teachers. By regressive I mean that preschool teachers end up thinking their main job is limited to preparing students for the real life of elementary school, while elementary teachers prepare students for middle school, middle school teachers prepare students for high school, and high school teachers end up preparing students for the Real World itself—unless, of course, the student goes on to college, in which case the job of preparing continues to be passed on. Everything is preparing; nothing is living. My job in this scheme of things, presumably, is to prepare my students to get jobs as first-year English teachers, and the record shows that I, in fact, do that. But if I narrowed my teaching practice to focusing on that outcome, my students would graduate knowing a lot about the discourse of teaching, interviewing, self-promoting, goal setting, and getting real nervous, but very little about teaching or living the teacher's life. My job—and every teacher's job—is much more than preparation: it is living at home with my students in the here-and-now of teaching practice. Now, wherever we are now, is what is important. This is how Dewey framed the issue:

> When preparation is made the controlling end, then the potentialities of the present are sacrificed to a suppositious future. When this

happens, the actual preparation for the future is missed or distorted. The ideal of using the present simply to get ready for the future contradicts itself. It omits, and even shuts out, the very conditions by which a person can be prepared for his future. We always live at the time we live and not at some other time, and only by extracting at each present time the full meaning of each present experience are we prepared for doing the same thing in the future. This is the only preparation which in the long run amounts to anything. ([1938] 1975, 49)

And here, again, is how Basho said the same thing:

> Each day is a journey
> and the journey itself, home.

Chapter Three

The First Pillar: Survive

The biggest question in nature is how to survive the year.
—Marty Stauffer, *Wild America*

George Kalamaras tells the story about the fish in the leech tank in order to illustrate the importance of openness and flexibility in teaching practice. However, there is a deeper and more primitive significance in what he has to say. Ultimately, the stories of the fish in the leech tank and the writing consultant in the biology department are stories of survival.

Survival, which most of us do not need to think about most of the time, is the most primitive drive. For all plants and animals it precedes all other concerns; it is the prime directive. Without survival nothing follows. This is as true in the world of the school as in the red-in-tooth-and-claw natural world. So it has always seemed ironic to me that the topic of survival does not come up often in textbooks, methods classes, and on-the-record conversations among teachers. At the university we usually do not have to face the primal, down-in-the-mud issues of survival that make up everyday life in the schools: the 160-student-a-day teaching load, the pregnant eighth grader, the kids with violent parents and police records, and the boys with guns in the trees out behind the school. But you can be sure that issues of survival do come up in the everyday thoughts and talk of teachers who live with these realities and who live each day in what are commonly referred to as "the trenches."

Talk about survival in education makes us uncomfortable at many levels. It conjures up images of "just getting by," of clock-watching teachers who cannot wait to get out the door in the afternoon and out on the golf course, or images of older teachers who have "given up" and are "just putting in their time" until they can retire. In many schools today, where there are weapons, gangs, and fights, survival takes on the most primitive and most original of meanings, totally stripped of any pretense or euphemistic jargon. To survive is to stay alive.

One of the reasons survival haunts me and surfaces as my First Pillar of teaching is that I did not survive as a secondary school teacher. True, I did complete two years, had some good experiences, and resigned by turning down a contract, but that is not enough. At best that is getting by. Survival is more than getting by. I wanted more for myself then, and I want more—much more—for my students and student teachers now. Survival is first. Survival is always first.

Failures

Educators are eternal—sometimes annoying—optimists and perennial tellers of success stories—often despite the facts. When they mention failure at all it tends to occur in the context of setting up a later account of success. Once, in a methods class, when we were reading a realistic account of a teacher's struggles, one of my students burst out with enthusiasm over having *finally* read something in a university course that seemed real and not contrived to present an idealized view of students or teaching practice. Her response only mildly surprised me.

For several years I lived where the local TV station televised the meetings of the school board. Since I had never been a frequenter of school board meetings, I was amazed at what I saw. Regardless of what they talked about, regardless of what problems were going on in the schools of the district, the board members and administrators seemed completely undisturbed. They generally smiled, were always polite, were always soft-spoken, and rarely disagreed with each other. This was due largely to the fact that they rarely addressed what seemed to me to be the most important issues facing them—issues like leaky roofs, large class sizes, inadequate professional release time for teachers, and the volume and frequency of stupid announcements on the intercom. What they seemed most concerned about was adopting special, creatively named programs proposed by men and women named Dr. This and Dr. That who came to the meetings wearing suits and equipped with overheads, color charts, and videotapes. My impression from watching the proceedings of this group was that at the top of the heap, in the boardroom and the conference room, no one ever fails and life is much more well regulated and antiseptic than it is in the place I know best, the classroom, where survival and failure cannot be dressed up and treated politely.

But failure is not something we should avoid, ignore, or be afraid of (even if many times we cannot help ourselves). Confronting failure, opening up to failure, even embracing it, can teach us many things about teaching and survival that are hard to learn in other ways. Therefore, at the risk of seeming negative, I want to briefly discuss four cases of student teachers who failed to survive. Even though it pains me to do this I hope that when I finish I am able to show that, even though each of these cases is different from the others, all of them have a common root that reveals an important and simple truth about survival.

The first failure was a young woman, about twenty-three or twenty-four years old, who was pregnant and student teaching in a small town. She was a very quiet and reserved person who was not quick on her feet, and her students literally hounded her out of the classroom. They would not be quiet and would not behave in an even remotely acceptable way, treating her with utter contempt. She took it passively, almost without acknowledging it. Despite the fact that her cooperating teacher and I supported her as much as we could and gave her specific directions on how to take countermeasures and disciplinary actions she could not, or would not, take them. The result was that she could not, or would not, stand up to her students and she was gone soon after midterm.

The second failure had a drug and alcohol problem. Before his student-teaching term began I was aware that something was not right with this student, and I tried everything I could to direct him out of the teacher education program. I failed at that because, despite his many problems, he managed to scrape by, meeting—barely—the published requirements for admission and continuance in the program. Once he was out student teaching, though, the situation rapidly deteriorated. From the beginning, his cooperating teacher reported to me that his attendance and arrival times at school were unpredictable and that his state of body and mind were not always stable. He would fly into rages at students or speak incoherently. His face was frequently florid or pale and his eyes looked alternately wild or dead. Very soon after he began student teaching I drove out to the school where he was and removed him.

The third failure was a middle-aged man who worked the night shift at a factory in order to support his family and put himself through school. All the qualities of character that my drinking and drug-using student lacked, this man had in abundance, and I respected his effort very much. With him I always wondered, though, why it was he wanted to become a teacher. He was not a particularly good writer, was not particularly articulate, and did not seem to be particularly interested in young people. All through the preliminary course work I repeatedly asked him to explain to me why he wanted to teach, but he never could. Still, he persisted. And sure enough, once out in the classroom he was confused, tongue-tied, and experienced strong anger and a contempt for his students that I had never seen before and have never seen since in the classroom. I still remember this scene: the student teacher standing at the desk in front of the class, face contorted, flushed, waving his fist in the air, and the students writhing in their desks, laughing, baiting him, defying him to be a teacher. He could not.

The fourth failure was a woman full of opinions. The high school she went to was the perfect high school, and the teachers she had were the perfect teachers. Everything she read, experienced, observed, or discussed in her course work she measured against the standard of her own experience and opinions. From the very beginning she had it all figured out and knew exactly what she would do and why that would be better than what any other teacher might be doing. Well, of course the predictable happened. When she finally began teaching nothing was the way she expected it to be, required it to be, in fact. The students were completely different than she had imagined, and nothing she attempted with her students—or in her relationships with other faculty members—worked. Her response was to persist stubbornly in her opinions and heap blame on everyone connected with the school. She was a zebra fish the leeches polished off in fine fashion.

What these four cases of failure all have in common is that each in its own way represents the point I was trying to articulate when I answered Rachel's question: that teaching practice is not just about the practice of teaching, but the practice of living. The first failure I discussed could not or would not stand up to bullies. The second could not stand up to his appetites. The third did not know himself, and the fourth could not bring herself to know others. None of these cases—or many others like them—involved any lack of specialized knowledge or required any particular kind of academic preparation. Book learning and study are important, but not enough. All the textbooks and all the education professors on the planet with all their knowledge could not have helped these people survive. And I certainly could not help them, though I tried as hard as I could.

This is not complicated. What I am talking about is learning how to live and living the life of a teacher. In the end, surviving as a teacher is not all that much different from surviving in any other profession or aspect of life. Everyone must learn the skillful means for living whatever life they are living. Surviving as a truck driver, surviving as a nuclear physicist, surviving as a spouse, or surviving as a minister require many similar qualities. In the section that follows I will take up six of these qualities and show how I believe they apply to living the life of a teacher.

Qualities for Survival

Know that teaching is what you want to do.

To oversimplify quite a bit, there are three kinds of students who come to me and want to be teachers. One kind is the kind of person who wants to be a teacher for all the wrong reasons, ranging from "I couldn't make it in engineering" to "My parents want me to have something to fall back on" to "What else am I going to do with an English major?" to "I like to read" or "I like kids." Unless such students somehow discover commitment and joy in the whole teaching life—which does happen—it can be sad to accompany them through methods courses and student teaching, to see them struggling with an unhappy or indifferent career choice, and to see them wandering off with confused looks on their faces when they are finished.

Another kind of student is the student who knows exactly what she or he wants to do, feels born to be a teacher, and enters the profession with a full-blown professional commitment. These are not students who come to teaching as a second choice or a last resort. These are students who have a strong calling to teach, and many of them, I suspect, could succeed without help from me or anyone like me. The third kind of student is the one who is somewhere in the middle between these two extremes, perhaps leaning toward becoming a teacher, but not yet certain and more than a little apprehensive. Jack Kornfield, a wise teacher in more ways than one, has this advice for anyone in this situation: "Always take the path with heart." This phrase comes from the work of Carlos Castaneda, in which he describes his teacher, a man named Don Juan, who tells him:

> Look at every path closely and deliberately. Try it as many times as you think necessary. Then ask yourself alone one question. This question is one that only a very old man asks. My benefactor told me about it once when I was young and my blood was too vigorous for me to understand it. Now I do understand it. I will tell you what it is: Does this path have a heart? If it does, the path is good. If it doesn't, it is of no use. (Kornfield 1993, 12)

Everyone, even the young with their vigorous blood, can understand what it is to feel and take the path with a heart.

The main hindrance to finding the path with a heart is the confusion and noisy mind that I described in Chapter 1 when I was telling the story of how I ended up jumping into the decision to teach. Dainin Katagiri, the Zen teacher I also mentioned in Chapter 1, suggests a way of moving through a noisy mind that I believe can create a context in which people with hard decisions to make might be able to position themselves to act in a more clear-minded manner. His way is based neither on the rational method of sorting out pros and cons (which works well in a great number of situations) nor on blindly jumping into the abyss, as I did. Katagiri's way is based on trying to reach the clarity and silence that lies at the center of confusion the way clear water abides in the stream and reappears once the turbulence of a passing animal or a storm has settled. He says:

> The opportunity for real silence occurs when we have been driven into a corner and simply cannot move an inch. This seems like a situation of complete despair, but this silence is quite different from despair. . . . [R]eal silence is that state of human existence that passes through this despair. (1988, 1)

Most of us, I think, can find a way to reach some level of clarity and silence in the process of living and making decisions, including the decision of whether or not to become a teacher. Look for ways of letting the conflict and argument go. Try to find ways of becoming aware of your noisy mind and what it is saying. Try listening to yourself. Do something mindless and repetitious. Go for a long run or walk or swim. Sew. Fish. Chop wood. Pray the same prayer over and over again until you can focus on it with fewer and fewer distractions. Concentrate on whatever action you are engaged in, and as you do, your mind may start to quiet down and you will see how it is that the problems and confusions you are having are not only problems with the decision itself, but also problems with mind. Focus on mind. Try to move through the conversation that is going on there. Take the time it takes to accomplish this: hours, days, more. If you can reach the point where the noise quiets and silence spreads, your heart will perhaps have an opportunity to speak, and you will be able to see what it is you want and need for yourself. In the case of teaching you will know that teaching is what you really want to do. Or not.

For me, these ideas only make sense when I think of them in terms of my basic, day-to-day practice. If I have a hard decision to make, it helps me to sit quietly, breathe easily, and focus on breathing. When my mind wanders, I try to bring it back to breathing. No matter how noisy and confused my mind is, I keep repeating this process. Eventually, perhaps after a long time, my mind finally will begin to settle down. When that happens, then it is possible for me to examine what is in my gut, what my heart is telling me, and what path it is directing me toward. Sometimes nothing will tell me anything, but I keep asking anyway.

Even though the general process I am describing here is based on Katagiri's practice, it is not, of course, the exclusive province just of teachers in his tradition. The need to find ways of answering difficult questions is universal. In Matthew's Gospel, for example, Jesus said, "Ask, and it shall be given you; seek, and ye shall find; knock, and it shall be opened unto you." That makes sense to me too. And in the Gnostic Gospel of Thomas, Jesus said, "If you bring forth what is within you, what you bring forth will save you. If you do not bring forth what is within you, what you do not bring forth will destroy you" (Pagels 1989, xv).

I want to make it clear that what I am talking about here is nothing more than a collection of broad principles for approaching the important decision of whether or not to become a teacher. I am not trying to prescribe formal methods for practicing Buddhist or Christian teachings. In Zen, zazen, sitting meditation, is not a technique for making decisions, finding the path with a heart, improving your life, preventing tooth decay, or doing anything. Zazen is just zazen. I do not think Christian prayer is designed for such uses either, although I do not know for sure. The reason my general approach as well as my personal technique for making decisions smells of Zen is because that is what feels most familiar and effective to me. It is not for everyone, though, and if you want to find a path with a heart, but do not like this way of doing it, go find another one. There is no shortage.

To survive you must be quick-witted, to be able to think on your feet.

Things happen fast in schools. Students are young, fast, and always in the flow of some action or conversation. In many ways they are products of the institutions that house them. The institution of the school is set up to *process* students, to move them around in large regimented groups, and everything is controlled by ringing bells, blowing whistles, group meals, and blaring loudspeakers. In order for the students to survive they need to be able to anticipate and outpace the system. To stay with the students, the teacher needs to be very quick indeed (unless the teacher has finally reached that happy point in life where she or he has become, like Jack Kerouac and Allen Ginsberg in Ginsberg's poem, "Sunflower Sutra," "tired and wily" enough to have outgrown the need for speed).

To be quick-witted means to be able to respond effectively and immediately to the constantly changing scene in the classroom. It means to be able to anticipate, to think one step ahead of the students. If your students are writing and one of them looks up and starts glancing around or leaning toward another, something is about to happen. . . . You can bet on it and had best be ready to respond to it.

To survive you must be slow and deliberate.

This is exactly the opposite of what I just said. As important as it is to be quick, it is just as important to be able to slow things down, to slow yourself down. If students come charging into class after lunch, it helps to slow them down. Reading to them or having them write for a few minutes can help accomplish this. Soothing music or soothing sounds help too. I remember once I went to visit a group of first graders on a day that my schedule was badly overloaded. I arrived barely on time and slightly out of breath just as the bell rang and the students came charging in after noon recess. The chaos was not good for me at that moment, so I was glad when the teacher announced "writing time" and all the students got out pencils and paper to write. I was just beginning to enjoy a quiet moment in which to regroup when the student nearest me turned and said in a very earnest voice, "You've got to write now." So I did, and by the time we had all finished, that classroom was a very peaceful place and everyone in it was ready to work.

There are two ways of responding when a student looks up in an adventuresome way and starts to initiate some action. One way is to be quick and proactive: give the student a look, clear your throat, get up and stand near his or her desk. (As is the case with real estate, three important factors in classroom management are location, location, and location.) Stay ahead, in other words. The other way is to be slow and deliberate. This means not to take action, except insofar as no action is a particular and very important kind of action. All the time students say little things or do little things to test the teacher, to get attention, or to initiate some minor skullduggery. Sometimes the best way of dealing with that kind of behavior is to ignore it, and it will go away. If it is something serious, though, and it does not go away, then it is time to move from action-as-nonaction to action-as-action.

Waiting and practicing nonaction apply to many more classroom situations than minor disturbances of the peace. Ask your students a question. If there is no response, wait. The pressure will start to build. It may seem as if nothing is happening, but something is. The students are getting uncomfortable with the silence. They are thinking about the question, too, formulating an answer even as discomfort and panic build in the room. In our busy, noisy lives, nonaction and silence stand out in significant ways. Something else is happening, too. Like your students, you are getting uncomfortable. The silence, in fact, may be much more uncomfortable for you than it is for your students. After all, noninvolvement might be their goal; it is not yours. Try to let go of the panic you feel and continue to wait, continue the silence. Eventually someone will crack. Hopefully it will be a student with an answer, which will help move the business at hand along. In too many instances, though, it is the teacher who cracks, answering the question and then proceeding to lecture for the rest of the class period, the semester, the year, a career, in order to avoid another episode of silence. Even if the teacher turns out to be the greatest lecturer in the world, the students get cheated out of participating in their own learning. And they get cheated out of silence.

Once I had a colleague who could always win this waiting game by maintaining silence for ten, fifteen, or even twenty minutes if necessary. I do not think I could wait that long unless I had the greatest question in the history of the universe hanging in the silence. My strategy more than likely would be to re-ask my question and revisit the silence again and again until something finally gelled. If nothing gelled I would let the question lie there like a dirty pair of sweat socks and move on. If a question is a truly good question it will come up again—maybe even on a test or in a writing task. Even if it does not come up again, my students at least might get the idea that I will not do their work for them—and that the questions will continue to keep coming.

To survive, you must be ready to take action.

What I am thinking about here does not necessarily have anything to do with quick or slow. Many beginning teachers are reluctant or afraid to take action—either proactively or reactively. They may fear a confrontation or be worried that someone will think they are not in control if they act in some conspicuous way such as assigning a student to detention or removing a student from class.

In a better world and in institutions that did not impose group behaviors on diverse individuals, there would be no problems that require unpleasant actions of any kind. But that is not the kind of world or the kind of institution in which most of us find ourselves. So, unfortunately for all of us, but especially for beginning teachers, serious conflicts with serious implications do arise. Indeed, nothing will get you run out of student teaching or removed from a job more quickly and surely than the inability to maintain "order," whatever that means to the administrators who are in charge of order. People who are in charge of administering large, complex institutions understandably love order. Some administrators will walk the halls of a school, and if the students in a particular classroom are quiet and well-behaved the administrator will perceive the teacher in that classroom as a good teacher—whether the students are learning anything or not.

It is also a fact that students will test beginning teachers. "Will the teacher stop me or can I get away with it?" The hard part is that if the student does get away with it, not only will that student be tempted to push the test further, the testing will spread to other students. Do not be afraid to stop students who are testing you. Here is how a student teacher described a situation in which he failed a test:

> Mr. [Cooperating Teacher] and I are "hall monitors" on the second floor for both lunch shifts. This job requires checking for passes and keeping the rest of the students behind the second-floor doors. This task seems simple enough but it is a good example of what I refer to

as "opening the floodgates." Each time a student sticks a head inside the door I immediately state the proper time to come up. They usually respond with a sigh and then close the door. This task is extremely easy, but on Wednesday of this week I showed up 5 minutes too late. The students were standing all around the doors with the doors wide open and students pushing their way closer and closer to coming onto the floor. By the time I got half of them back the bell had rung for them to come up. It seemed like no matter what I did or said they ignored me completely. All it took was one person to stand on the wrong side before everyone was doing it. Individually I could make them get back, but when there were ten students out of line they knew there was nothing I could fairly do to any one individual. . . .

This lack of ability [to deal with this situation] is partly caused by my lack of aggressive nature, but I have no problems dealing with students one on one. This fact makes it all the more important for me to squash misbehavior before it gets out of hand. Like the "floodgates," once I give them some lack of discipline, they all follow the leader. In short, this is a simple problem with a simple solution. But if that simple solution is delayed the problem becomes a big problem.

This student teacher is coming to a number of important realizations. First of all, I hope he realizes that showing up for a job five minutes late is a bad idea. A really bad idea. Second, he seems to be learning that, especially in dealing with large numbers of students, action cannot wait. Most beginning teachers have less trouble dealing with students one on one than in bunches. If this student teacher had been in position on time he probably could have dealt with problem student number one individually and the complications would not have multiplied. Third, he seems to be discovering that one of the main ways students test beginning teachers is by ignoring them. In many ways open defiance is much easier to deal with. When someone defies you lines are clearly drawn, and it is relatively easy to know when to act and even how. But ignoring is much more subtle, harder to interpret, and harder to document. "What, me? I wasn't doing anything. I thought the bell had rung and it was OK for us to be on second floor . . . Yaddah, yaddah, yaddah." Finally, and perhaps most important, this student teacher is beginning to understand important truths about himself. "This lack of ability . . . is partly due to my lack of aggressive nature." Even the sentence he writes here does not want to take a stand and state forthrightly that he "isn't aggressive" or even that he "lets people push him around." He is learning things about himself, but slowly, tentatively, perhaps too tentatively. Teachers—anyone who must deal with large groups of people—must be "aggressive." I do not mean here that teachers must be aggressive in a combative sense like military drill instructors or riot police—although it is nice to have people like that around the school. What I mean is that teachers must know how to make a stand, to make a point, and *manage* students when it is necessary. One of the most effective managers of students I know is a soft-spoken female teacher who stands five feet tall and weighs just over a hundred pounds. She can turn the blood of the most unruly students to ice with little more than a glance. Once I asked her what her secret was. She said matter-of-factly, "Oh, I used to play in a rock band in sleazy bars, and there you have to know how to deal with problem children." I also know a male teacher who used to play defensive tackle for a Big 10 football team and who once overpowered and disarmed, without injuring, a student who was bent on violence. Action is action.

Before I continue, I would like to mention why students in the previous example were not allowed on the second floor during lunch. The reason was to give the teachers some privacy in the middle of the day. The second floor was closed to students so teachers on their lunch break would have a quiet place to work, to reflect, and to walk the long, spacious hallways in order to get exercise in much the same way that walkers go to malls before the stores open. Even though this may seem unusual and a selfish use of space on the part of the teachers, it is important to keep in mind how closely confined and circumscribed the teaching day is and how important even a few minutes of exercise, collegiality, and quiet can be in helping enhance the quality of one's work and work experience. The hall monitor had an important job with implications for many people, and he should not have let them down.

Next, I want to turn to an example of another student teacher who was faced with a management problem and managed to move herself to take action:

> I was confronted with an anxiety I hoped I could avoid. A boy in my . . . English class gave me no choice but to prove my authority. I sent him to the office for misbehavior.
>
> It all took place during a lesson over rhyme and meter. By its very nature, this subject matter is hard to comprehend. But to deepen the heartache, a few boys in the class kept making "smart" comments, which in turn got the class riled up. My approach was initially to ignore it.
>
> But then it escalated. Warnings shot out of my mouth left and right. Still no luck. I had a choice: let the students who misbehaved take control or I take control. I opted for the latter.
>
> I sent one of the "leaders" to the office. I simply told him to get out of the classroom. The students know they are supposed to go see the principal when these things happen.
>
> Afterwards, I felt guilty. I kept thinking if there wasn't something I could have done to prevent that step. But after thinking about it I realized I made the right decision for two major reasons: 1) the student

was invading other students' rights to an education, and 2) I had to
show I would keep my promise to carry out my warnings.
      While I still regard sending kids to the office a final resort, I am a
little less reluctant to do it because I realize it can both help students
who do behave and help me to regain control of the classroom. (Tremmel 1993, 452)

This was written by a student teacher in a desperate situation. Not
only had she been having discipline problems in her classes, but the
school she was working in was having discipline problems too: there was
tension between faculty and administration, political tension among
faculty members, and a general lack of collegiality and mutual support.
Even though the student teacher had been encouraged by her cooperating teacher and by me several times to remove this particular student
from her class, she did not do so because she feared the response of administrators and disliked having to resort to such a measure, which she
interpreted as a sign of failure. Finally, she did send the student to the
office.

      For this student teacher, survival became a pressing need in a
threatening environment, and she took action. "I was confronted with
an anxiety," she begins. She does not begin by saying that she was confronted with an unruly student. This seems significant to me, because
many teachers' first inclination in such a situation would be to put the
blame "out there" on the student. Not so in this case. Consciously or
unconsciously, this student teacher knows right from the start that
finding and applying the appropriate means of discipline is only part of
her challenge; she knows that an equally important part is for her to
recognize and pay close attention to her own anxious state of mind,
which arises as a reaction to her students' behavior and is an index of
the threat she feels.

      She knows she is in deep trouble and in the midst of a painful
situation that is escalating out of control. She understands that she is
losing control of herself by getting as "riled up" as her students, and
that loss is a significant part of the situation. "Warnings shot out of my
mouth left and right" is a powerful figure of speech that suggests a loss
of control. When this student teacher says, "I had a choice: let the students . . . take control or I take control. I opted for the latter," she is not
simply saying that she took control of the class, but that her decision to
send the student to the office also helped her regain control of herself.

      This is not to imply, of course, that when teachers decide to take ac-
tion, the need to survive should always lead to a confrontation with a
student followed by throwing the student out of class on his or her ear.
On the contrary, it is a good practice never to get involved in a confrontation with a student, especially in front of the student's peers or
classmates. The teacher will always lose that one, because the student's

ego will be on the line and the student will feel the need to stand and fight. Much better to remove the student from the situation, to talk with her or him quietly in a corner of the room or outside in the hall. Many times this turns out to be a way for students to escape from a bind they have gotten themselves into, as well a quiet way for the teacher to resolve a problem she or he is having, too. However, if a student is incorrigible, disruptive, belligerent, threatening, cursing, or violent and will not settle down, then that student must go. No doubt about it. Nothing can happen in class for the rest of the students unless the problem is removed.

Many teacher educators tell their student teachers that they should never throw a student out of class. I agree that removal is always a last resort, but there are times when it can cut through impossible knots of problems and is the best thing for everyone concerned—even though it may take a great deal of time for the situation to clarify itself fully. What I am getting at here goes back to the law of karma, which holds that action necessarily creates results and the need for more action. This means that when you take action in class—especially removing a student—the process is far from over. Instead, it has just begun.

One of the few things I succeeded at as a high school teacher was inventing what I think of now as "high-impact" detention. When I took serious disciplinary action, such as removing a student from class, I required that the student come to my classroom after school rather than go to some detention hall or other warehouse facility. And when we were together we would talk. And talk. And talk. One hour, two hours—I did not care. I would ask the student questions about his or her life, interests, school experiences. I would inflict long motivational monologues. It was brutal. But it was also good. Students in high-impact detention learned two things in a hurry. One was that the last thing in the world they ever wanted to do again was sit for two hours on a nice spring afternoon and discuss the meaning of life with Bob Tremmel. The second thing, paradoxically, was that they came to get the idea that for some mysterious reason Bob Tremmel was interested in them. Granted, he was a strange, harsh, and unpleasant guy, but in his own way he did care and was fairly decent about it after a few hours. When students who had been in one or more sessions of high-impact detention returned to class, they acted differently, with more care, and that spread to their classmates—who did not necessarily want to have the Bob Tremmel-after-school-experience. Everyone benefitted.

Perhaps even more significantly, high-impact detention had high impact on me, too. One of the first students I went through this process with was named Wally. Wally made me as angry as any human being has ever made me. He was defiant, he was arrogant, he was crude, and he was dangerous. To put it mildly, I did not like Wally very much and

Wally did not like me very much. Our first after-school session started out as an hour-long argument and shouting match. When the initial burst of anger was spent, though, something unexpected began to happen. We began talking with each other. Wally began telling me things and—to my surprise—I started listening to him. I listened to what he had to say about my shortcomings, his many unpleasant experiences in school, his sense of failure, his family, his aspirations. Over a period of hours and days, with him talking and me listening, Wally became transformed in my eyes from an unruly clod bent on destroying me to a real human being I wanted to help. This was a powerful experience for me. From that moment on, I never saw my students the same way again.

I still remember the year after Wally had graduated, joined the army, and returned home after basic training. My room overlooked the parking lot and the front door of the school. I saw Wally's car pull up and I saw him get out, dressed in his pressed green uniform, wearing a tie, a garrison cap, and very shiny shoes. I watched him proudly stride up to the entrance and pass under the portico, and I wondered what in the world he was doing at school. Seconds later Wally appeared at my door with a huge, proud, shining smile on his face. No matter what my other failures were, and no matter how heavy the weight of them hung on me, in that moment I felt like some kind of teacher.

When you take action with a student there is a commitment forged that requires loyalty and from which there can be no honorable retreat. This is particularly true in the case of removing a student from class. Of course, the first follow-up in that situation is with the administrator in charge of discipline—usually the principal in a small school or an assistant principal in a large school. Without exception your administrator should support you. If not, then it may be time to look for a new job. Ideally, after the principal visits with the student and comes to some kind of initial decision about the disposition of the case, the three of you should also have a talk and put in place some kind of plan to help the student rejoin the class. Many times it is useful to bring the parents into this process. Sometimes—if the student's home situation is contributing to the problem—it is not. Sometimes it may turn out that the student will not come back to your class if the problem is such a serious one that the student is suspended or expelled from school. This is an especially serious action with especially serious consequences. No one wants to see a student thrown out of school. But it does happen and it often turns out in surprising ways.

When my son (whom I used to call "sideswiper" because of his unique driving abilities) was in high school he got into some trouble with the law and was put on probation. He was a very troubled young man. As luck would have it, the probation officer to whom he was assigned had also been a very troubled young man when he was in school—so troubled, in fact, that he had been expelled. After a few years of knocking around and failing to get a good job, in desperation he entered a G.E.D. program and earned his high school diploma. After working for a couple years he was admitted to college, then was awarded a scholarship for academic excellence, earned his degree, and became a probation officer. He helped my son and many other young people in ways even they will not fully understand for several years. Today, this ex-failure, ex-delinquent, ex-probation officer is in law school and claims that the best thing that ever happened to him was being expelled from school. So there you are. When is not surviving, surviving? When is surviving, prevailing? From action—even apparently bad action—much good can flow.

Be your own teacher.

To be your own teacher means two things. First, it means the same thing we mean when we tell people to stand on their own two feet and to "be your own man" or "be your own woman." It means to think for yourself, act on your own, take responsibility for your life, and practice self-reliance. In his essay titled "Self Reliance" Emerson wrote:

> Let a Stoic open the resources of man and tell men they are not leaning willows, but can and must detach themselves; that with the exercise of self-trust, new powers shall appear; that a man is the word made flesh, born to shed healing to the nations; that he should be ashamed of our compassion, and that the moment he acts for himself, tossing the laws, the books, idolatries and customs out of the window, we pity him no more but thank and revere him;—and that teacher shall restore the life of man to splendor and make his name clear to all history. ([1841] 1966, 53)

In this Emersonian sense, to be your own teacher means not to be controlled by textbooks, curriculums, professional organizations, or by anybody or anything. Mind you, I am not saying that it means to *reject out of hand* textbooks, curriculums, and professional organizations, all of which are important to the functioning of the school and have the potential to contribute to our development as teachers. I am saying we should not be controlled by them.

Once I was in a classroom watching a teacher conduct a lesson on a short story her students had just read out of a textbook. It was pathetic. There she sat at the front of the room with the teacher's edition of the textbook open on her lap while she asked the proverbial questions "listed at the end of the story." When a student answered, she would carefully check that answer against the answer in the teacher's key, tell the student either "correct" or "incorrect," and then mark in her grade book. No discussion, no engagement, no one at home. She was definitely not her own teacher, if she was a teacher at all.

Second, "be your own teacher" means to learn how to teach yourself what you need to know to develop professionally and to grow in your teaching practice. Finally, if we are serious about our lives and our practice, we come to the realization that there is only so much that other people—scholars, researchers, supervisors, teachers, friends, colleagues—can do for us. At some point, even though we do not abandon our respect and our willingness to learn from others, we must move out on our own. At some point we must realize deeply for ourselves that even though we might not always travel alone, the journey we are on is our own journey and no one else's. Once I had a student teacher whose greatest desire was to go back and student teach in the high school she graduated from with the teacher she had there who was, in her mind, the ideal English teacher. Even though I was strongly opposed to her doing this, and even though the university had a strict policy against student teachers teaching in schools they had attended, somehow she and her family pulled the right (or the wrong) strings and she got what she wanted.

It is true that we often get what we deserve when we get what we want. Back in the presence of her ideal teacher in her ideal school, she immediately tried to copy his methods and mannerisms. It was a poor and a pale imitation and she knew it. This realization plunged her into cycles of frustration and feelings of failure "to measure up" that resulted in intense suffering for all of us. Who knows what kind of teacher she would have been if she had not limited herself by hoping to become a teacher she could never be in a world that no longer existed. Much better for her and for all of us to be able to let go of who we were and who we think we are and live the practice and the life that can be ours and no other. What we had is not what we have now and what we have now cannot last. Our old teachers' lessons fall on ears that no longer hear. Much better to be our own teachers in the present moment and nowhere else.

Study yourself, know yourself.

These are ideas about self that have been around a long time and that represent to all people in all cultures bits of the most profound wisdom concerning survival that we are capable of attaining. Plato, in the dialogue titled *Phaedrus,* has the student Phaedrus ask Socrates whether or not he believes in myths and mythical characters. In replying, Socrates brushes aside the superficial thrust of this question before adding in a more serious tone that:

I myself certainly have no time for . . . [this] . . . business, and I'll tell you why, my friend. I can't as yet "know myself," as the oracle at Delphi enjoins, and so long as that ignorance remains it seems to me ridiculous to inquire into extraneous matters. Consequently I don't bother about such things, but accept the current beliefs about them, and direct my inquiries, as I have just said, rather to myself. (1961b, 478)

Around 1,700 years after the time of Plato, in thirteenth-century Japan, the Zen teacher Eihei Dogen wrote in a similar vein that to "Study the Way is to study the self" (Yasutani 1996, 35; Tanahashi 1985, 70). And in seventeenth-century England, Thomas Browne, a physician and scholar, echoed the words of both Plato and Dogen when he found in self-knowledge a godly and goodly virtue. In "Religio Medici" ("Religion of a Doctor") Browne wrote:

He is wise, because He knows all things; and He knoweth all things, because He made them all: but His greatest knowledge is in comprehending *that* He made not, that is, Himself. And this is also the greatest knowledge in man. For this do I honor my own profession, and embrace the Counsel even of the Devil himself: had he read such a Lecture in Paradise as he did at Delphos, we had better known ourselves, nor had we stood in fear to know *Him*. ([1643] 1937, 263)

In the same essay, in a section devoted to charity, Browne elaborated on this point by writing of a particularly important form of self-knowledge. "But how shall we expect Charity toward others," he wrote, "when we are uncharitable to ourselves? 'Charity begins at home,' is the voice of the world; yet is every man his greatest enemy, and, as it were, his own Executioner" (317). The phrase "Charity begins at home" and the ideas behind it have worked themselves so thoroughly into our popular vernacular that I worry we tend to overlook their crucial importance, their wisdom, and the true difficulty of applying them to our lives. "Know your limitations," the coach tells the player, "and play within yourself." "Try to discover what it is you really want to do," says the employment counselor. "Be good to yourself," say the English educator and the talk radio shrink. "Only you know what's best for yourself," I tell my students all the time.

But how do we know these things? Why are they so important? And, perhaps most significant, what particular skills or practices can we learn that will lead us to self-knowledge? Everyone is full of all kinds of fragrant aphorisms about these matters, but how many of us both know for ourselves and know how to teach our students to go about this particular process of learning?

A sad and frustrating part of my job is to see people enter the profession who have everything it takes to become good teachers but who cannot survive because they cannot find a way to know self in a way that creates a comfortable balance between the demands of professional life and personal life. Several years ago, new to an area, I visited a school for the first time. No one there had seen anyone from my university for several years. Almost the first thing the teachers and the administrators in this school talked with me about was an English teacher, call her Linda, who had taught there several years before, who had graduated from the university where I worked, and who had been the best teacher any of them had ever known. Even though it had been a long time since they had seen her, everyone's eyes glowed as they recalled this teacher. But when I tried to find out where she was and what had happened that had caused her to leave, I was met with downcast eyes and shaking heads. "Burned out in four years," they said. "Tried to do the job she knew had to be done and that she knew she could do, and just flat burned out."

As these things sometimes develop, several years after this encounter I had a chance to meet this extraordinary teacher. After resigning her position Linda left the profession altogether and went on to become successful as the director of a social services program organized to help struggling families survive. Sadly, but happily too, she found a way to follow her calling to support and aid others in an institution that was set up differently than the institution of the school, an institution that, while far from perfect, offered her the possibility of succeeding, surviving, and living at the same time.

And what kind of institution is the school and how did it contribute to the end of Linda's career? As you might imagine, the answer to this question has many sides to it. One side that I think is relevant to the issue of survival centers on the changes in schooling that took place one hundred years ago with the consolidation of independent rural schools into large government-run bureaucracies. This process was a leap into the unknown at the time, and the professional educators driving the process, whose jobs and reputations were on the line, turned for guidance to the only models of large institutions they had available: business, industry, and the military. As a result, the consolidated and urbanized schools ended up becoming institutions governed by hierarchies that functioned autocratically in a top-down fashion, often with minimal input and oversight from teachers, students, and the community.

The school of today has not changed much. It is still an institution run like a business that mass produces education by departmentalizing and compartmentalizing learning according to subject matter and turns out products called "graduates" as efficiently and as inexpensively as possible. It is commercialized in every way, from the high-priced products that textbook and media companies sell to teachers, administrators, and school boards to the concern that the "products" the system turns out will be "productive." One aspect of this productivity is the need for graduates to carry with them a minimum of intellectual baggage that might complicate the functioning of other institutions by causing the graduates as employees to ask questions and cause trouble for employers. So, one of the things students learn first and learn thoroughly is that if they want to succeed in the system they should sit still, shut up, and do what the authorities tell them—and teachers must likewise learn how to labor and survive as replaceable components in a system that values them too little and over which they have little control. This setup, I can only say, is truly strange.

Now, I know that this is only one side of the school, and a dark one at that, but I think it is the side of the institution that has the potential to drive good teachers like Linda out of the profession. When she first became a teacher she committed herself, body and soul together, to her students and their learning. She worked twelve-, sixteen-, eighteen-, twenty-hour days. She worked wonders of the sort that are too rarely worked in the schools. And just as the mountain will allow hikers to go as far as they want and not care a bit what happens when they go too far, neither does the institution do a good job of protecting those whose commitment is particularly intense. The classes Linda taught were too large, the number of preparations she had was too many, the amount of work it took to do a good job was too great. Where other teachers would have pulled back and settled for less, this teacher pushed on, could not figure out a way to survive, and finally left.

The question that begs to be answered here is how, all at the same time, can you survive in the institution of the school as it exists today, succeed in living a full life, establish a full teaching practice, and, perhaps most important, get into a position where you can shine some light on the darker sides of the institution? Learning how to breathe helps. Learning how to shop, as Sally Hudson-Ross did, also helps, as do the six qualities for survival I have discussed in this chapter. The following three points, I believe, are also worth considering in this context.

Surviving Is Living

Charity begins at home.

Thomas Browne was right. This is a simple concept, but a difficult one for serious people to grasp. If you are working so hard that you are falling asleep on your way to work in the morning, if you are losing weight or making yourself sick, or if you are watching your relationships fall apart because of the time and effort you are putting into your teaching practice (or your practice as a student, or both), give yourself a break. Do not be afraid to admit to yourself what is happening to you. And do not think that if you take a night off or get enough sleep that you are beginning down a slippery slope to mediocrity. Very serious people do not become mediocre teachers or mediocre anything else. And if you have a tendency to do and do and overdo that is too strong to deal with alone, do not be afraid to find someone who can help you understand what is happening with you. (Those of you who are reading this and do not know what I am talking about, get up off the couch, throw your TV out the window, quit procrastinating, and get to work!)

Cultivate life-giving practices.

Overworking, underworking, overusing alcohol or food, or pursuing other unhealthy addictions are not life giving. They are killers. So is runaway stress, fear, and anxiety. All of these things lead to illness, perhaps serious illness, which could ultimately kill you. So, if the stress of school or the job or the institution begins to wear you down or if you begin experiencing fear or pain, the first thing is to get help: medical help, counseling help, religious help. Help. Sickness is not an outcome of professional life over which we have no control.

For most people such serious measures are not necessary, and everyone can develop many life-giving practices that can help them take care of themselves before they get in trouble. It seems like a cliche to talk about the importance of pastimes and hobbies, but they are important. I know many teachers who are athletes, gardeners, hunters, musicians, collectors, and players. Such pursuits are life giving. Even more basic is to build a solid physical foundation for your life. Good diet is important, exercise is important, stress-reducing practices are important, and all of these function together in a life-giving way. I know a teacher who is in her mid-fifties and who has one of the toughest jobs in an urban high school. Most of her students are at-risk students, and many come from homes and neighborhoods that are falling apart and afflicted by substance abuse problems, gangs, and violence. Her work is an inspiration for me, and of all the aspects of her practice that I admire, what I admire most is the way she conducts her life outside of school and how the life she is living supports her professional practice and helps her survive.

And what is this life that she is living? She rises early and eats well, primarily vegetarian dishes with an emphasis on whole grains and fresh, unprocessed food, although she likes pizza, too. She exercises by running and walking. She used to be a competitive distance runner, but now her goal appears to be primarily fitness. She has a very active intellectual and social life: she reads; she writes; she attends concerts, films, and poetry readings. She maintains spiritual, mental, and physical practices based on meditation, stretching, and yoga that not only support her other life-giving practices and disciplines but make it possible for her to move with strength and flexibility through the difficulties of the institution where she works and the confusion of her students' lives and problems.

Good living is not limited to this kind of lifestyle, though. I know a teacher with a completely different approach. He too is in his fifties and has taught for many years. Instead of concerts and poetry readings he enjoys popular literature and sporting events, and instead of vegetables and whole grains—rabbit food, he calls it—he likes burgers, fried cheese sticks, and a few beers on a Friday afternoon. However, even if on the surface his way of living seems very different from the other teacher's way, underneath he works to accomplish the same things: a balance of mental, intellectual, physical, and leisure activities carried on in a conscious way and with awareness of building an integrated life that supports his teaching—just as teaching supports and helps give meaning to his life. If he were a student of Basho or Dogen, which he is not, he might begin to recognize in the kind of life he is trying to live certain aspects of what, since the time of Buddha, has been known as the Middle Way. Balance. Integration. Centeredness. Not too much of one thing; not too much of the other.

When I visit the first teacher in her urban school, she sometimes starts class off by ringing a bright-sounding bell, the sort of bell used in monasteries to signal the start of meditation or prayer. The music of it is very calming. When I visit the second teacher in his suburban school, we go on the "nature walk" during lunch period. Our walk takes us out the west door, around the building, into the north door, and back to his classroom. The trip is refreshing even though it is short. These are small things, perhaps, but when combined with other life-giving practices they add up to something very significant. Balance. Integration. Centeredness.

These two very different people with two very different approaches to living and teaching are both survivors. They are both intensely alive in their teaching practice, and any student teacher who works with either one of them had better be prepared to commit fully to teaching and living, to approaching each day with courage and dedication, and to serving students. And these teachers expect no less from me, either.

Leave school at school.

One natural outcome of developing a balanced, integrated life is an increased ability to live in the moment. So much of people's lives is spent living in the future by planning or daydreaming or worrying, or in the past by stewing or regretting or reliving anger. It is easy to wear out very rapidly if you carry such inner turmoil with you twenty-four hours a day. Both the teachers I have mentioned, or any other survivor, have in common the ability—most of the time—to leave whatever has happened to them or with them behind and to move on. "Lock it up in your classroom," you hear teachers say. "Leave it at school." Or, as I tell my students, "Keep moving or you will be wounded." There are leeches all over—real and imagined—that will catch you and suck the life out of you if they can manage to stay with you long enough.

Chapter Four

The Second Pillar: Pay Attention

How do we know what we think we know? How do we know if it is any good? One traditional way that professionals in many fields have "made knowledge" is through "research" and "scholarship," which are used to create "theory," which is then dispensed to practitioners who are responsible for "applying" it in their daily work. In education this process has usually begun with researchers and theorists in universities who write articles and books that are studied by teacher educators. The teacher educators, then, follow up with more research and theories before delivering the results of all this labor to classroom teachers, whose job it is to figure out how to put it into practice. Traditionally, teacher educators have considered theory and their role in making knowledge to have many virtues and uses. Here is a passage from a famous English methods textbook written by James Moffett and Betty Jane Wagner:

> Faced with thirty or so wrigglers in a room, you may grow quickly impatient with theory. But good theory should serve as a blueprint for action so that you *know* what to do Monday and any other time. It should provide a basic framework that indicates what to do in any situation, and why to do this rather than that. It does not guide, however, by spelling out action as specifically as a musical score or a recipe. It gives you a comprehensive and integrated perspective within which all problems can be placed, a consistent way of thinking so that you can think what to do as you go. (1983, 2)

At the time this was written, the relationship between theory and practice seemed simple and clear-cut: theorists made theory and other forms of knowledge and then made them available for practitioners to interpret and implement. When I was failing as a practitioner I listened to what the knowledge makers told me to do and then tried to figure out ways to do it. The outcome was bad, but I was not deterred. When I started teaching methods courses and supervising student teachers I changed roles and became a middleman in this semicommercial arrangement, giving my students theories and then helping them figure out ways of enacting the theories in the classroom. This did not turn out very well either, but I was still not deterred since I believed in the system and had a tremendous amount of faith in the power of theory and the need for practice to follow after it.

As long as everyone involved in this discipline-wide system was able to sustain their faith in theory guiding practice, it seemed as if there were no serious problems—even if what the experts said often proved to be less than expert. But what gradually happened was that increasing numbers of people began waking up to the fact that there always seemed to be annoying disparities between theory and practice, between "ought" and "is," and that many theories were not much more useful for guiding practice than Ptolemy's theory of an Earth-centered universe turned out to be for guiding space shots. Postmodern scholars and educators, adept at deconstructing well-established theoretical edifices, were particularly instrumental in this process of awakening, as were English educators like John Mayher (1990) and even Moffett (1994) himself. In many ways it began when an unconventional rhetorician and compositionist, Stephen North, said out loud and in public what no one in the Age-of-Faith-in-Theory would ever have thought to say: that in the theory-into-practice system the experience and relative worth of teachers was ignored, and that the knowledge emerging from teaching practice itself—what North called "lore"—was held in low esteem compared to the status granted to the knowledge produced by theorists and researchers. One of the conclusions North reached was that this way of doing business, in which teachers were not listened to, was backwards, and that it would make sense to take the knowledge of teachers more seriously. North was not even afraid to suggest that faith-in-theory had been misplaced from the beginning and that theory was not as important as everyone had always thought. Speaking of the teaching of composition North wrote:

> Given the sort of treatment they have suffered, it may seem a little ironic that, in fact, practitioners have been responsible for composition holding together as long as it has. But they have been and remain just that: at the center of the field's knowledge making explosion, exerting a sort of epistemological gravitational pull, there has always been the enormous inertial mass of lore. (1987, 371)

North's questioning of the traditional way of looking at theory and practice did not go unchallenged, but it attracted sufficient attention to contribute to the growing uncertainty of both theorists and practitioners in the way they understood how they should interact with each other. Views like North's and the debates that have followed from them have left teacher educators and teachers in a curious position. For years it was easy to explain teaching practice in terms of proper respect for theory and the need for teachers to be theoretical in the way Moffett and Wagner prescribed. "Without theory," I can still hear myself saying to my methods students, who were surely tired of hearing it, "we will all be doomed to chaos and bad Monday mornings." As time went on, though, and as I became more and more convinced that such an approach would no longer suffice, the question of what should replace it pressed closer and closer. It was one thing to read books, go to conferences, and listen in on the increasingly strident dialogue over this question. It was another thing altogether, though, when my students turned to me for answers, and I struggled with my doubt, my sense of failure, and the nagging sense that I was failing to give them what they needed.

From Theory to Perspective

This is the question: If faith-in-theory is no longer the best way for teachers to follow, what way is? Or, to put it another way, what is it that teachers need to know and where is the best place for that knowledge to come from? One way of beginning to get an answer for these questions is in the way Ann Ruggles Gere, Colleen Fairbanks, Alan Howes, Laura Roop, and David Schaafsma frame the theory-practice-knowledge problem in a book they have written titled *Language and Reflection: An Integrated Approach to Teaching English*. This is a book my students and I use in one of our methods classes. In the view of these authors we should give up looking at single broad theories as having a foundational claim to authority, and instead consider each theory locally and in terms of its own merits as a "perspective" or "approach" to teaching.

The authors of *Language and Reflection* name four of these perspectives. The first is "language as artifact," a text-centered approach in which the text and the teacher's interpretation are most important. The second is "language as development," a cognitive growth approach that features "modeling" and "scaffolding" and in which materials and activities are based on the students' levels of ability. The third is "language as expression," an approach in which primary importance is attached to students' personal and collaborative experiences with writing and texts. The fourth is "language as social construct," a postmodern approach based on ideas that emphasize the importance of real-life experience, community action, political awareness and activism, and collaboration.

Ann Gere and her colleagues do not argue for any particular approach. They present each one and then point out what they think are its strengths and weaknesses. "You must develop a theory of your own," they tell beginning teachers (1992, 84). Since, as I said earlier, I think it is important for all of us to "become our own teachers," I like this advice. However, like all advice, including mine, it is dangerous. One danger, for example, is that beginning teachers coming in contact with all these theoretical "perspectives" will respond as if they were at a salad bar and begin choosing a little of this and a little of that from overlapping or contradictory theories and practices. Sometimes building such concoctions works out just fine in the classroom, but other times there are confusions. Once I had a student teacher who found it very appealing to let her students ask their own questions and come to their own personal interpretations of the texts they were reading as they might in the "language as expression" approach. When the students were done with their questioning and interpreting, however, the student teacher switched perspectives, as one might go from the lettuce to the macaroni salad, and began lecturing her students on her own interpretation and explaining to them what was wrong with theirs. In her view, all she was doing was making a very legitimate shift in her perspective to "language as artifact," but it is easy to guess what happened the next time she asked her students to start off by expressing their own views: nothing. They knew what was coming.

Reflection

In the broad view of the authors of *Language and Reflection* we find ourselves in a pluralistic world where the practitioner is freed from serious commitment to any single creed or foundational dogma. Where Moffett and Wagner developed a comprehensive theory as a guide for practice, the authors of *Language and Reflection* provide a variety of theories for survival in a profession that is changing and diversifying just like the culture in which it exists. They do something else, too, which turns out to be significant for all of us in this discipline. They include a third term in the discussion of theory and practice: "reflection." They see reflection as an analytical tool for selecting and developing a theoretical position. In a chapter titled "Becoming an English Teacher: Theory into Practice," they write:

> Developing a theory of language and learning out of which you can shape your classroom and reflecting on that theory in practice keeps

you an active learner in the continuing process of your own education; it also enables you to develop a questioning, critical posture about teaching.

And as we begin to find our way, we must *reflect* on our teaching practices so that we continually change and improve our theory. Theory and practice should exist in a reciprocal relationship in the process of learning about teaching. (60)

This view of theory, practice, and reflection moves quite a distance from a simple pattern of teachers' receiving theory from outside sources and then putting it into practice. Instead, here teachers may begin with a theoretical perspective, but then reflect on their own teaching in order to assume a more active role as they enter into an ongoing creative process of theory-into-practice-into-theory.

Of course, the idea of reflection was not invented by the authors of *Language and Reflection*. Indeed, someone might argue that the last sentence in the passage from Moffett and Wagner that I quoted previously, where they say that theory provides "a consistent way of thinking so that you can think what to do as you go," represents as much of an approach to "reflecting" on theory and practice as the approach outlined by the authors of *Language and Reflection*.

Another earlier—though by no means the earliest—use of the term "reflection" comes from the work of Donald Schon, someone well known to the authors of *Language and Reflection*. Schon has for years been very interested in professional practice and how professionals, including teachers, learn to practice as professionals. In his book *The Reflective Practitioner*, Schon begins by describing a "crisis of confidence in professional knowledge," which he attributes to "technical rationality," the "dominant epistemology of practice" in the education of professionals (1983, 21). He means that the various professions like medicine, law, business, and education get their official knowledge of how to do what they do from theories that have been created technically and scientifically outside the realm of practice and are then passed from thinkers to doers. This is not necessarily a good thing when it comes to education, because what technical rationality tends to produce are rules and step-by-step models of behavior that often do not really match up very well with what is going on in the nontechnical, nonrational, and sometimes-throw-the-rule-book-out-the-window world of the classroom.

Now, neither Schon nor any other reasonable person would say that technically rational thinking is bad or that we can live without it. Many of us, in fact, would not be alive today if it were not for theories developed by researchers in such fields as chemistry, physics, agriculture, and medicine. What Schon is saying is that single-minded attachment to this one kind of knowledge making leads to a destructive tendency to separate the authorities and sources of knowledge from knowledgeable practice. This in turn leads to the mistaken notion that knowledge gained by scientific research and represented in the form of theories is the best—or even the only proper—knowledge available for us to use when we respond to the challenges of practice.

According to Schon, knowledge gained from technical rationality may be important, but it does not provide enough basis for practitioners who are operating in what he calls the "swampy lowland where situations are confusing messes incapable of technical solution" (45). Learning to traverse this swampy lowland calls for a kind of knowledge that reaches beyond the knowledge available from the methods of technical rationality. Schon explains this kind of knowledge by introducing what he calls "knowing-in-action" (45). Knowing-in-action is know-how. Unlike knowing from technical rationality, knowing-in-action cannot be reduced to theoretical constructs, analytic formulas, or narrow specifications of behavior. Knowing-in-action goes beyond what we can say we know to what we know but cannot say.

For Schon, the processes that underlie such knowing are "reflecting-in-action" and "reflecting-on-action." Schon's notion of reflection seems disturbingly simple and anticipates where I am headed in this chapter. He compares it with thinking on your feet and talks about it in terms of "noticing" what it is you are doing in practice, getting a "feel" for it, and simultaneously adjusting your practice (56–61). One example he uses to illustrate knowing- and reflecting-in-action is the practice of baseball pitchers. First of all, Schon quotes what some baseball people have said about the way pitchers come to know what they are doing through such processes as "finding the groove":

> "Only a few pitchers can control the whole game with pure physical ability. The rest have to learn to adjust once they're out there. If they can't, they're dead ducks."

> "[You get] a special feel for the ball, a kind of command that lets you repeat the exact same thing you did before that proved successful."

> "Finding your groove has to do with studying those winning habits and trying to repeat them every time you perform." (54)

Of the pitcher's reflective practice, then, Schon goes on to say:

> I do not wholly understand what it means to "find the groove." It is clear, however, that the pitchers are talking about a particular kind of reflection. What is "learning to adjust once you're out there"? Presumably it involves noticing how you have been pitching to the batters and how well it has been working, and on the basis of those thoughts and observations, changing the way you have been doing it. . . . The pitchers seem to be talking about a kind of reflection on their patterns

of action, on the situations in which they are performing, and on the know-how in their performance. They are reflecting *on* action and, in some cases, reflecting *in* action. (54)

A second example Schon uses, and it is easy to imagine how he frames it, is of jazz musicians who are improvising and making up their own music as they go. Even though such musicians are working from some established line or chart, what they really come to know about the music they are making comes from the action of making it. There are grooves in jazz, too.

Teacher Research

Moving from reflection in baseball and jazz to the classroom is a step that those of us who are interested in Schon's ideas are eager to make, but have difficulty doing while maintaining contact with Schon's bottom line and the direct simplicity of attention. This is most obvious in the way educators have applied "reflection" in the teacher research movement. "Teacher research" or "classroom research" or "action research" is a method of knowledge making that gives teachers authority over their own practicing and theorizing. In teacher research, the main idea is that each teacher knows the problems and issues in her or his own classroom better than anyone else, so it should be up to the teacher as a teacher-researcher to explore those problems, research them, and then come up with answers that, along with other answers from other sources, can help the teacher build theory and practice from the ground up in the teacher's own natural setting. Teacher research is such a compelling idea in the educational knowledge-building business that university researchers like Sally Hudson-Ross and Curt Dudley-Marling are going back to teach in the schools in order to be able to speak authoritatively about what is going on there.

Reflection, understood as "systematic, theoretically informed, deliberate reflection" (Dudley-Marling 1997, xiii), is a key part of the processes of teacher research. For example, Eleanor Kutz, in her book about teacher research, describes a model that seeks to move her student teachers from a state of being "unconfident answer-knowers" to "more confident question-askers" (1992, 68). The process of being engaged in this professional development, Kutz says, "provides a way of constructing and revising a personally-situated theory of teaching and learning, one that both emerges from and informs examined practice" (69). Her claim for this system is that it produces the "sort of theory that can best support beginning teachers as they encounter new contexts"

(69). In order to help accomplish all of this, Kutz's student teachers keep extensive teaching journals in which they "reflect" on experience and put their evolving theories into "examined practice" (73, 75).

Here is what this sophisticated-sounding process looks like. Following is the last paragraph from a longer passage in which one of Kutz's student teachers "reflects" on his experience in the process of "evolving theory into practice":

> I had them read the last paragraph of chapter 4 [in *To Kill a Mockingbird*], and I read it aloud, dramatically! They got it, the tension and stuff, so I asked, "All right, what do you think is going to happen? There are a lot of pages left in this novel, and based on what you've read, speculate on the plot development." Well, they dug that. We all talked; each student responded. When one student said, "I don't know," I said, "Neither do I, but what do you think might happen?" They all participated. (73)

On the basis of reflections like these, Kutz concludes that this beginning teacher is able to reflect on practice, theorize, and finally "create a larger model of effective classroom discourse" in the form of statements like the following, which is taken from a further reflective writing:

> Never say "wrong," say "why do you think that?", "explain that to me please." The students teach themselves this way. . . . I think students learn most effectively when they come up with both questions and answers. (74)

Two other English educators, Joy Ritchie and David Wilson, also emphasize the importance of students and teachers acting as researchers and reflecting in order to build up their own approaches to teaching. In addition, they see the knowledge that teachers gain from reflecting as central to the process of becoming able to enter self-sufficiently into the professional discussion and to take strong, enlightened stances on professional issues. Ritchie and Wilson say that beginning teachers must have

> opportunities to reflect critically on their experiences . . . to delve into the assumptions on which those classrooms are based, to set those assumptions in dialogue. . . . By reclaiming and reflecting on their own histories as readers and writers, and then extending that reflection outward [beginning teachers] might become participant observers of language and learning around them, and so go on to confront reductionist views of education and provoke questions for themselves that clarify their own purposes for education. (1993, 82)

What Kutz, Ritchie, Wilson, Dudley-Marling, and other advocates of reflection in teacher research are after with ideas like these is a way of encouraging teachers to use their own critical powers in order to make sense of practice experience and build theories that can act as the further basis for practice.

Key to this process is the ability of individuals to detach from the action they are engaged in and thereby gain a perspective that leads them to insight, knowledge, and eventual transformation. This is not easy, and the activities implied by detaching yourself from what you are doing raise some tough questions. For example, if you detach yourself, from whom are you detaching? Who is the detached person watching? Who is really doing the watching of what and whom? How do you learn the skills and disciplines for such a complex mental activity in the context of your first teaching experiences when your stress level is off the scale and you may feel overwhelmed by factors and forces beyond your control? And how did the processes of reflection get so far away from Schon's baseball pitchers and musicians who reflect and build knowledge, not by detaching but by moving deeper and deeper *in*—by becoming immersed in practice so that they can exert close, intuitive control over their actions? *Moving in* is one thing. *Detaching* is something else.

Stanley Fish, another baseball fan and scholar, is an outspoken critic of reflection-as-detachment. He links these ideas with various states of mind like "critical self-consciousness" and "critical self-reflection" (1989, 457, 609, 610) and labels them as basically ridiculous. The big problem for those who promote detached reflection in the form of "critical self-reflection," Fish says, is the contradictory belief that, on the one hand, everyone constructs knowledge in personal, social, and historical contexts, but that, on the other hand, it is possible to disengage at will from those contexts and engage in objective, critical acts of reflection. This view, Fish goes on,

> seems to me to be zany because it simply assumes but never explains an ability to perform that distancing act, never pausing to identify that ability and to link the possession of that ability with the thesis of the general historicity of all human efforts. That is, most people who come to the point of talking about critical self-consciousness or reflective equilibrium or being aware of the status of one's own discourse are also persons who believe strongly in the historical and socially constructed nature of reality; but somehow, at a certain moment in the argument, they are able to marry this belief in social constructedness with a belief in the possibility of stepping back from what has been socially constructed or stepping back from one's self. I don't know how they manage this. I think, in fact, that they manage it by not recognizing the contradiction. (266)

This skeptical view aims right at the foundation of teacher research, systematic reflection, and other related ideas about how to understand theory, practice, and what is happening in the classroom. If we buy into them, where do the contradictions Fish identifies leave us? Years ago, by relying on theory, we had basic principles to guide us in our teaching practice and professional lives. Without theory, methods like reflection and teacher research seemed to hold promise for giving us power to act intelligently and to create practical and conceptual knowledge in the actions of teaching. But if theory is not to be trusted and if reflection and teacher research seem to involve questionable—or even "zany"—elements, to what source should we turn to find out what it is we need to know?

Two Persons in One Self

At the center of Fish's objections to critical self reflection lies his dissatisfaction with a process based on two persons in one self—a reflector and a reflectee, we might say. The desire to split the self like this goes back a long way in the history of human thought and is connected with the absorbing interest human beings seem to have in establishing all kinds of dividing lines between mind and body, subject and object, individual self and others. It is only by thinking along such lines that it is even possible to conceive of such acts of mind as critical self-reflection, objectivity, and detachment.

A good early example of this way of thinking comes from Plato's dialogue, *Phaedo,* where he has Socrates comment on the ideas of absolute truth, beauty, and goodness. Plato wrote:

> Surely the soul can best reflect when it is free of all distractions such as hearing or sight or pain or pleasure of any kind—that is, when it ignores the body and becomes as far as possible independent, avoiding all physical contacts and associations as much as it can, in its search for reality. . . . Isn't it true that in any inquiry you are likely to attain more nearly to knowledge of your object in proportion to the care and accuracy with which you have prepared yourself to understand that object in itself. . . . Don't you think that the person who is most likely to succeed in this attempt most perfectly is the one who approaches each object, as far as possible, with the unaided intellect, without taking account of any sense of sight in his thinking, or dragging any other sense into his reasoning—the man who pursues the truth by applying his pure and unadulterated thought to the pure and unadulterated object, cutting himself off as much as possible from his eyes and ears and virtually all the rest of his body, as an impediment which by its presence prevents the soul from attaining to truth and clear thinking? (1961a, 48)

Here, Plato takes the idea of splitting the self all the way, drawing lines of separation that not only set the self off from other people and objects, but also set mind against body, self against itself. Even though this way of thinking may make some people like Stanley Fish uncomfortable, and even though I have a hard time conceiving why anyone would want to dissect human nature in such a manner, Plato's approach does work. Western culture, in fact, is proof of that, since so much of what we have and how we operate is based directly on similar approaches to splitting the self. Religious systems, for example, rest on whole series of creative splits and distinctions: spirit vs. flesh, good vs. evil, Heaven vs. Hell. Likewise, our science operates on the similar basis of methods that involve an "objective" or detached observer or researcher who stands apart from and manipulates research subjects, objects, equipment, and data. We can also see this pattern in other institutions as well, including legal and governmental structures based on opposition, confrontation, hierarchy, check-and-balance. Even though it is fashionable in these days of "New Age" ideas to attack Western culture for such tendencies toward dualistic thinking, the record shows that this use of mind has been a potent tool for building great civilizations and comfortable, technologically advanced democracies.

It should not be so hard to believe, then, that on a smaller scale dualistic thinking can also be a potent tool for teacher research and reflective practice. Educational literature is full of testimonials that show people can and do separate mental functions and senses of self, as well as shift perceptual and conceptual roles with others and even with themselves. Whether Fish can accept it or not, Kutz's student functions in this manner, and my students do it all the time too. Indeed, going back to Schon's seminal ideas about reflective practice, what, besides an ability to think dualistically, could make it possible to reflect-*on*-practice in the first place?

Mindfulness

To some people, a defense of dualistic thinking may seem like an inconsistent argument to find in a book based in part on Zen, which has the reputation of being a quintessentially nondualistic discipline. Nevertheless, I really do think that splitting the self, thinking dualistically, and reflecting-on-action can help all of us do better jobs in the classroom, and it is the classroom I am concerned about and not the apparent philosophical purity of this book. However, I also think, along with Fish, that dualistic ways of thinking and knowledge making have limitations and can trick us into thinking we know a lot more than we really do. What Kutz's student learned in his act of reflection may have been true and may well be useful knowledge on which to base future actions. On the other hand, every teacher knows it is easy to get into situations where it is not possible for students to "teach themselves" in the way he concludes, and the next time he tries it he may get nailed. Consequently, I do confess I am eager at this point to move beyond the dualistic, and often problematic, side of reflective practice toward a more single-minded understanding.

When Basho wrote "Each day is a journey, and the journey itself, home," he was not thinking dualistically, nor was he reflecting-on-action. Rather, I believe he was representing, in a way consistent with his practice and his culture, a view of nature and experience not dissimilar to what Schon was trying to get at with his view of the single, integrated reflective practitioner who is "doing one thing and not two" (1987, 22). This is reflection-*in*-action. For Basho, journey and home are one thing and not two. The traveler is one person and not two. For Schon, when it comes to reflecting-in-action, thinking and doing, thinking and being are not separate acts. This is an important point because it provides a view of reflection that balances out—not cancels out—the effects of the dualistic and pulls body, mind, subject, object to wholeness. This is also an important point because it gets us back to the level of directness and simplicity that made Schon's ideas about reflection useful in the first place.

Here is an old story that illustrates what I mean. This particular version is taken from Philip Kapleau's book *The Three Pillars of Zen:*

> One day a man of the people said to Zen Master Ikkyu: "Master, will you please write for me some maxims of the highest wisdom?"
>
> Ikkyu immediately took his brush and wrote the word, "Attention."
>
> "Is that all?" asked the man, "will you not add something more?"
>
> Ikkyu then wrote twice running, "Attention." "Attention."
>
> "Well," remarked the man rather irritably. "I really don't see much depth or subtlety in what you have just written."
>
> Then Ikkyu wrote the same word three times running: "Attention." "Attention." "Attention."
>
> Half angered, the man demanded: "What does that word 'attention' mean anyway?"
>
> And Ikkyu answered gently, "Attention means attention." (1980, 10)

The simple way of understanding reflective practice is to understand it as "paying attention." "Paying attention" means to be fully present in your life and your teaching practice. It calls on you to use the total range of your abilities: physical, mental, spiritual. Paying attention means to see, to hear, to touch, to taste, to smell, to look closely, to perceive details, to notice your thinking whenever, however, and wherever it occurs. Paying attention means to attend to what is happening to and with your students and to attend to what is happening to and with you, your thoughts, actions, reactions, feelings from one moment to the next. Paying attention is not to split off or "think about"; it is to move deeply into the action—even, paradoxically, when that action is to "think about" by reflecting-on-practice.

Howard Tinberg, a community college English teacher, arrives at a point similar to mine by a different route. Tinberg says that neither the issues of theory and practice nor the other problems of teaching will ever be resolved until we teachers move beyond our distractions and take charge of our attention in the classroom. "To observe our classroom," Tinberg says, "is to reclaim it, [and] in observing our observations we teachers will find ourselves both inside and outside the setting we are studying. . . . We . . . must study ourselves as we study others" (1991, 41). For Tinberg, studying the self is not merely a matter of detachment, but a more inclusive matter of staying in the scene and studying the self under all circumstances. Tinberg's metaphor for this, which he borrows from Louis Aggassiz, is "seeing" (43). Make no mistake about it. This too is a very simple notion that integrates the myriad forms and concepts of reflection-in- and reflection-on-action.

In Zen, paying attention is often referred to as "mindfulness." It is a practice that has been around for a long time. Kazuaki Tanahashi, who translated the thirteenth-century Zen Master Dogen's writings, points to mindfulness as central in Dogen's Zen teaching:

> Zen meditation—sometimes described as mindfulness . . .—is done sitting upright in a cross-legged position. Dogen teaches that this practice . . . is not merely a method by which one reaches awakening, but is itself awakening. (1985, 12)

"Mindfulness" extends Schon's ideas about reflection and Tinberg's "seeing" to encompass the whole practice of living. Thich Nhat Hanh, a Vietnamese Zen Buddhist monk, who is surely not caught up in Plato's dislike of the body, writes:

> The Sutra of mindfulness says, "When walking the practitioner must be conscious that he is walking. When sitting, the practitioner must be conscious that he is sitting. . . . No matter what position one's body is in, the practitioner must be conscious of that position. Practicing thus the practitioner lives in direct and constant mindfulness of the body. . . . " The mindfulness of the positions of one's body is not enough, however. We must be conscious of each breath, each movement, every thought and feeling, everything which has any relation to ourselves. ([1975] 1987, 7 see also *Transformation and Healing: Sutra on the Four Establishments of Mindfulness*)

The purpose of mindfulness, as much as it can be said to have a purpose, is not to analyze experience or thought processes, or to evaluate, but to help the practitioner "study the mind" (see Dogen and Uchiyama [1243] 1985, xi). This means to come to know and understand the mind in a direct and immediate way that is not automatically accessible with analysis or evaluation or Dudley-Marling's "theoretical reflection." Shunryu Suzuki describes mindfulness this way:

> The important thing in our understanding is to have a smooth, free thinking way of observation. We have to think and to observe things without stagnation. We should accept things as they are without difficulty. Our mind should be soft and open enough to understand things as they are. . . . Thinking which is divided in many ways is not true thinking. Concentration should be present in our thinking. This is mindfulness. (1970, 115)

Despite the fact that such points of view sometimes have the reputation of being esoteric, this view of mindfulness represents a very direct and concrete approach to experience. Mindfulness moves away from absorption in the endless, noisy parade of thoughts through the mind. Mindfulness also helps reintegrate the divided mind/divided self that operates in critical self-reflection. When one is mindful, one lives in the present and pays attention—pure and simple. Dainin Katagiri writes:

> When you walk on the street, be mindful of walking. Mindfulness is to go toward the center of whatever you are doing. Usually the mind is going in many directions; instead of going out in all directions, let's go in. This means, look at the walking you are doing now. (1988, 30)

Even though the term *mindfulness* is most closely associated with its 2,500-year heritage in Eastern disciplines, it is easily accessible to Westerners. For example, in a book titled *Mindfulness*, based on psychological research, Ellen Langer draws a distinction between what she calls "mindfulness" and "mindlessness." She defines "mindlessness" as thought and action entrapped by rigid categories and habitual and "automatic behavior." According to Langer, one particular form of mindlessness that plagues education is an "outcome orientation" that forces attention away from present "processes" and toward fixed requirements for the future: once an outcome is determined, it becomes possible to stop thinking much at all about what one is doing and why one is doing it—except as it bears on the end preordained by the outcome. To act only according to outcomes or future goals, as Langer and John Dewey both point out, is to act mindlessly. (It is, of course, equally mindless to act without reference to any plans or goals. Nothing is either *this* or *that*.)

In contrast, Langer's idea of "mindfulness" pictures an open mind that focuses on the processes of thought and action in the present, on "awareness of the processes of making real choices along the way"

(1989, 75). Although Langer is correct to state that her idea of mindfulness differs in significant ways from ideas of mindfulness in Eastern disciplines, she does acknowledge sharing with those disciplines an understanding of mind that is in-action and in-process, and that is not bound by the "old categories" and "rigid distinctions" (79) that are by-products not only of mindlessness, but, as Schon would surely agree, of overreliance on technical rationality as well.

Even though "paying attention" and "mindfulness" are very simple ideas to grasp, they are not so simple to practice. On the other hand, they are not impossible to practice either, as Fish fears is the case with "critical self-reflection." In Zen, mindfulness begins with the practice of sitting meditation that I described earlier. It is a posture that supports concentration and awareness. Back is straight, head is aligned with body in an overall posture that is neither rigid nor slack. Eyes are open, but unfocused on the wall in front. Attention is focused on breathing and posture, and the mind is awake, aware, but loose and flexible. When thoughts come up and the mind wanders off after them—and the mind always wants to wander—we let them go and return attention to the here and now of breathing and sitting. This returning, time after time as the mind wanders off and wanders off, helps us locate the center of mindfulness.

Mindfulness in the Classroom

Mindfulness, returning, attention are not limited to sitting. If they were, Zen and other meditative disciplines in all the cultures of the world would be merely forms of escapism. Instead, mindfulness, returning, attention are carried over into other activities, first to active forms of meditation, like walking, yoga, and martial arts, and from there to everyday tasks of all sorts. When you sit, sit. When you walk, walk. When you teach a class, teach a class. The "reflective practitioners" Schon describes and the "see-ers" and teachers Tinberg knows are intimately familiar with the practices of mindfulness, returning, attention whether they have ever sat down on a cushion and faced a wall or not.

These reflective practitioners, like Zen students, even benefit from paying close attention to posture and position. One reason for this has to do with physical survival. Very often in stressful situations—and teaching inevitably involves stressful situations—people's muscles get tense and tight, which contorts their bodies into curious and uncomfortable positions that they may or may not notice. The result of this is pain: sore shoulders, sore neck, headache, back pain. Being mindful of bodily posture and condition can help you monitor how you are doing physically and adopt postures that are upright, yet loose enough for you to remain comfortable.

On those days I work on campus instead of in the schools, I climb three flights of stairs until I reach the floor where the main office of the English Department is. I always stop by this floor on the way up two more flights to my own office in order to pick up mail and conduct other business. After leaving the stairs and walking down the hall I pass the office of one of my colleagues, a very intense, hard-working person. When I pass by this office I often look in the door and see my colleague working, getting ready for class. Often I notice this person's body is in an awkward position, as if the upper torso were involved in some activity independent of the lower torso. The result is a hurried, twisted, shape that suggests attention being in two places rather than one. I often find myself doing exactly the same thing, and it does not surprise me a bit that many times over the last several years I have heard this colleague mention pain in various body parts. How much better off we are if we take time and pay attention to our posture and face straight ahead, focusing mind and body in one place, not two.

Mindfulness of posture and conscious taking of posture can help in other ways that are familiar to experienced teachers. If you are in a position where you need to "deliver the word" to your students for some reason, you are likely to take a formal, standing posture at the front of the room. If you want your students to relax, you might want to sit casually in a desk chair or on your desk. If you want students to take over more responsibility in the classroom, you would move to the side or the back. Once I had a student in a methods class who taught a short lesson to her classmates. The posture she took was sitting on a chair in the front of the room with one foot on the floor with the other up on the chair seat. Even though she was wearing blue jeans at the time, and even though the posture might have been comfortable and appropriate for a college student, it was definitely not the kind of posture useful for a teacher. What surprised me most, though, was that after she finished, despite being able to recall everything her classmates had said during her teaching, she had no recollection of what her posture had been. If we do not practice mindfulness, returning, attention, it is amazing what slips by.

One teacher I know is particularly skilled at paying attention. Her classroom is somewhat unusual. The students' desks are arranged in concentric circles with an open space in the middle and three aisles that run like spokes out from the center. The teacher has no desk. Instead, she moves around the room, sitting in empty desks, on extra chairs, or standing and talking with her students individually, in small groups, or all together. When I first went to visit her in her classroom I was somewhat taken aback. I arrived during a class, located the teacher, gave her a wave when she looked up, and then stood off to the side waiting for her to finish her conversation with a student. After her initial acknowledgment she did not even once look my way for twenty minutes. The student was having problems with a piece of writing, and she had the teacher's full attention. Although I could tell the whole time I waited that the teacher was monitoring the other students who were in the room, she was very deeply absorbed in her talk with the one student. Her alert posture showed her attention, her eyes showed her attention, and her disinterest in distractions like me showed her attention. Since I had not met this teacher before, it might have been possible for me to take offense at her lack of attention to me, and if she had been rude to me later on I might have done just that. But when the time came for her to talk with me she gave me exactly the same full attention that she gave her students. Even though much of attention is an invisible, internal, mental process, it shows. Everyone knows when someone is paying attention.

When teachers are able to open themselves and practice mindfulness, returning, attention with their students and with themselves, sometimes very interesting things occur. For the first time, perhaps, they begin to see what is actually happening, how they are operating in the classroom with students, and how the students are receiving the teaching. Sometimes coming to be able to see such things can be unpleasant: sometimes teachers see that they are not doing such a good job. Sometimes coming to be able to see leads teachers to big changes in their practices and their lives.

One of my favorite books about teaching is titled *In the Middle*. The author is Nancie Atwell, a middle school teacher. The book opens with the story of how, early in her teaching career, Atwell was focused more on the particular teaching methods she was using and on her own opinions about teaching than she was on what was actually happening with herself and her students. As the years went on, though, and she became more and more able to practice her version of mindfulness, returning, attention she became increasingly able to see her students and herself, and as a result her teaching practice and her whole life changed.

Attention is central to Atwell's teaching practice. This is obvious in every word she says throughout both editions of her classic book about teaching reading and writing to middle school students. Her basic way of responding to students' writing, for example, is a one-on-one conference in which Atwell goes to her students, not the other way around. She conducts conferences with a small footstool to sit on, a clipboard for keeping records, and a pad of Post-it notes for making nonintrusive responses and demonstrations. Her main emphasis is on reading and listening to students and waiting until she has taken in what she needs to know in order to help. Her attention is directed 100 percent to her students, and her main concern is with asking the right question and finding the right response for the right student at the right time. "Make eye contact with the writer," she writes in the first edition. "This means kneeling or sitting along-side their desks as you talk and listen" (1987, 94). In the second edition she elaborates, "Strive for balance between listening to students discuss their writing; listening as they read aloud texts that are relatively brief . . . or passages from longer works; and, after the writer has told you what he or she wants help with, reading their texts silently to yourself" (1998, 225). Mindfulness, returning, attention: fundamental, basic skills of teaching practice. I remember the one time I met Nancie Atwell. It was in Pittsburgh at a conference and she was speaking in a hotel ballroom with a raised dais and a podium at the front. When Atwell started she was standing at the podium, but after forty-five minutes or so she finished and the large audience began to separate into smaller discussion groups at the corners of the ballroom. I noticed that for a moment during this transition Atwell was alone on the dais, and since I had a question to ask her I seized the opportunity. When I approached she was standing about three feet above me. I was able to catch her attention and, feeling somewhat uncomfortable, managed to say something like, "Could I ask you one quick question?" I am not sure what I expected her to do or say, but what happened next totally surprised me. She turned toward me, moved directly to the edge of the dais, and in one single, sweeping motion bent down and put her face directly in front of mine at eye level. In that instant I knew clearly that I had her full attention, and the effect of that was so overwhelming that I almost could not speak. It is so rare, I think, to be given full attention—especially in public settings—that when it happens we do not know what to do. For students with a teacher like Atwell, the attention they receive during conversations and conferences must stand out in the school day as very special times.

The following story is another example of what I mean. It is told by a ninth-grade teacher who has been practicing mindfulness, returning, attention at a local Zen center for several years. She says:

> Right now I have a very troubled student in my at-risk class, who has been coming to class daily and sleeping. She's depressed, she doesn't make eye contact, she puts her head down on the desk as soon as she gets there. She's aware of what's going on and isn't actually sleeping, but she appears to be, and she doesn't participate at all. The other teachers who talk about her complain about this. Apparently she has a troubled household and she's absent—emotionally absent—most of the time. One day recently I decided that I would put myself in her shoes, and what I observed was her body language. I decided to just approach her physically, so I put my hand on her shoulder and leaned over and said, "Do you feel alright? Would you like to go to the nurse?" And her response was to sort of brighten up, a real change in the pattern of behavior that had been common with her.

For me, in that moment, there was suddenly a change in the way I was able to see, a focusing of attention that I associate with the rhythms of [mindfulness] practice. Suddenly, it was possible for me to do what I had not been able to do before—to read her body language, read her need. It wasn't what I ended up doing that struck me the most, but the kind of attention I was paying to the moment, the way I was taking the situation in. It wasn't just, "Well, I should be nice and go over and see if she wants to go see the nurse." It went beyond that in my feeling toward her, and I think that she picked up on that. I think there was a different moment between us because I could forget everything else going on in the classroom—just for five seconds or ten seconds—and be fully present for that one student.

You know, this is hard to do if you have thirty kids in the class, to do one thing at a time. This is true in our culture at large, and I— and I may be prejudiced here—but I think this is particularly true for women. It's difficult because we are taught to juggle as much as we can do at once. You know, the baby on the left hip, the phone in the right hand, stirring dinner at the same time, and feeding the cat. And so it almost feels like a luxury of some kind or a laziness to do only one thing at a time, to pay attention fully to doing the dishes without also listening to a documentary and trying to do several things at once. But it's been through my Zen practice that, first of all, I was introduced to, and then came to see the value of, doing mindfully one thing at a time. And that's what I was very aware of doing with this one particular student in the one particular moment to which I'm referring.

Slices of Classroom Life

I would now like to illustrate some other ways mindfulness, returning, attention function in the classroom by discussing four short writings by teachers and student teachers. These writings are what I call, for want of a better term perhaps, "slices of classroom life." When I assign my students slices of life I ask them for a writing that is divided into two parts. Part one is given over to the detailed narration of some specific and limited "event" in school and is to be written in the form of a "thick description" similar to the field notes of anthropologists who look closely and write in detail in the process of investigation. Part two, then, is given over to what Schon calls reflecting-on-action, to writing about the thoughts, feelings, and speculations that arose during and after the event. Taken together, part one and part two represent a combined external and internal survey of teaching practice, thoughts, and feelings. Writing and thinking in the terms required by slices are particularly useful activities for us as teachers because they encourage us to practice paying attention and provide an opportunity to stand back in the process of writing and thinking to attend to the action.

Slice 1

All teachers, but especially beginning teachers, find it difficult to pay attention. Sometimes at the very beginning the problem is simply fear. One student teacher wrote in a slice of life about her first time in front of the class. The students had just finished reading silently and she was preparing to have them read aloud and then discuss:

> As I watched the students finish their reading, an insane buzz filled my head, my blood pressure probably hit its highest, and I tried to get them to draw the first connection between the poetry [and an article they had read earlier]. I stalled, and had a volunteer read the first two stanzas [of the poem]. Some angelic looking child took pity on me and read. After she read, I fumbled out the first question. . . . I think I got nervous waiting for answers; I rushed past some students' answers when I could've made them fit, and finally just felt totally lost to that buzz filling my head.

How well I know that buzz! I still remember my first class, my first day on the job as a high school teacher. It was 8:00 A.M., a bell rang, and the room filled up with strangers who sat down and looked to the front of the room at someone who must have seemed even stranger to them. I remember that at some point I began speaking. My voice sounded to me as if it were emanating from somewhere above and slightly to the left of the pencil sharpener at the back of the room. The buzz filled my head and the room became foggy, grey, almost dark. I am sure I was very close to passing out.

This fear and this buzzing, although they may seem like very significant experiences, are really nothing more than the physical and mental manifestations of abject terror. I mention this here in order to show that certain states of extreme mental agitation make truly paying attention difficult, if not impossible. Even though experienced teachers are not likely to have fear like this—since over time most of us learn that fear is truly nothing to be afraid of—all teachers every now and then must deal with serious distractions that affect their presence in the classroom: sickness, a sick child, a death, a failing relationship. Under conditions like these all we can do is the best we can do, and work to regain attention.

Slice 2

In addition to big things, sometimes it is difficult to pay attention when small things intrude on us, too. When life in the classroom does not go well and we get angry, frustrated, upset, it is easy to get lost in these feelings. (The same thing can happen when life goes extremely well. Ecstasy can be as big a distraction as fear or anger.) The following slice of life illustrates some of these problems. It was written by a student teacher working in a middle school classroom. This teacher was having an experience that many beginning student teachers may not expect to encounter but do.

> On Wednesday I was explaining their writing assignment to them and they all had a handout that explained the assignment; however, I did not put everything on the handout. I wanted them to take some notes so they might remember the details better. I told them when I handed it out that I wanted them to take notes and that they would need a pen or pencil. They all got a writing utensil, but very few students were writing anything down. So I hinted by saying "this is important" and finally "write this down." Still about a third of the class did not move. Then I felt the pressure of the whole day and I said sarcastically something to the effect that writing involves picking up your pen and making marks on the page. My tone of voice finally sparked them to action and finally they were all paying attention and were receiving needed information.
>
> I am learning every day that seventh graders are really little kids yet. Getting them to engage in thinking or even listening is very difficult. It seems like I have to give detailed explanations over and over. It seems like there is no valve that keeps information in the brain. What goes in one ear comes out the other. And what is in the brain comes out the mouth. There are no stops. I feel frustrated a lot because I feel like dealing with all of that gets in the way of my objectives of what I want them to actually learn. I suppose I will get used to their personalities as I get to know them and then it will be easier to ignore what now gets in the way.

In the first part of this excerpt the student teacher shows that she is able to pay attention to much of what is happening in her classroom with her students. She is aware first of all that her students are themselves having an attention problem. Furthermore, she is also aware of the escalating increments of action she has to take in order to begin to get her students' attention. In addition, and this I believe is most important, she is aware that her actions and perceptions are connected to how she feels about the way her day has gone. This is important because it helps keep her mindful that what she perceives happening in the classroom is strongly conditioned by her feelings and what she makes of them.

But it is in part two that the importance of attention becomes clearest. The metaphor she uses for teaching and learning reveals a lot about how she sees her students and her role as teacher. In this metaphor the students are defective, mechanized containers of some sort without the necessary valves and stops to keep in the information she (pours?) (injects?) (infuses?) into them. Playing out this metaphor leads to the humorous, cartoonlike image of the teacher running madly around trying to stop up leaks, put her finger in the dike, etc. Reinforcing this metaphor is her comment that the students are getting in the way of her objectives for them, as if teacher and students are antagonists set against each other in an anti-learning process.

For this student teacher, this slice of life became a way not only for her to pay closer attention to her students, but to herself too. It was surprising and disturbing for her to see how her way of seeing students as containers removed them as active participants in their own learning and reduced learning to passive reception of information. She was particularly unhappy with herself that she had on her own come up with a variation of Paulo Freire's "banking" metaphor for education "in which the students are the depositories and the teacher is the depositor . . . in which the scope of action allowed the students extends only as far as receiving, filing, and storing deposits" ([1970] 1992, 58). Likewise, the student teacher was also surprised to note how far she had gone toward focusing her teaching not on her students but on herself in the need she felt to fulfill lesson plans and meet objectives. It was also disturbing for me, as her supervisor and mentor, to have this slice of life force my attention on how my own emphasis on lesson planning and classroom organization had helped to unbalance a beginning teacher's practice. Both of us, clearly, had to find a way to return our attention to our point of central focus—the seventh graders. But how hard it is to pay attention to what is going on around us! How hard it is to attend to what is going on even closer to home!

Slices 3 and 4

The next two slices of life help me return to the issue with which I began this chapter, the relationship between theory and practice. The first slice was written by an experienced teacher in a college freshman composition program. It describes a situation in which a white student comes to the teacher and questions the inclusion of African American and Hispanic literature on the syllabus. The student tells how, because of her background, she feels fearful of students from other ethnic groups. She goes on to suggest that since America is supposed to be a "melting pot" of many cultures it is not necessary to study specific minorities and their literatures. What follows is an excerpt in which the teacher reflects on her encounter with her student:

> One reason that we study the works of minorities in the classroom is precisely because of the reason for her sense of fear. I explained that there is a connection between racism and ethnicity, and that racism is often just a case of ignorance. . . . To elaborate I said that since we, as Americans, come from different backgrounds, it is this difference that makes a polyethnic society rather than a melting pot. I validated my

point by asking her if her family had certain traditions, say, for instance, during the holidays. . . . After this response I proceeded to expound on more crucial topics such as what civil rights means.

The next slice comes from a student teacher who was working with a group of tenth graders reading *Romeo and Juliet*. In the last few minutes of the class the student teacher asked her students to read a short scene on their own and write a plot summary. One of the students refused to write. This led to a confrontation that the student teacher describes before she goes on to say:

> I finally got him to write a very brief summary of what he knew so far—but I pulled him aside after class and I just said, "Bob, we're going to have to get through this and I don't want us to end up enemies over it." Well, I think he had a pretty bad day or something because this upset him terribly. He informed me that he didn't give a shit about school or Shakespeare, or anything and he started to leave. I followed him and said, "Bob, don't leave. Let's talk about this," and he whipped around with tears in his eyes and said, "You don't have any idea of the problems I've had." He was almost fierce and it scared me.
>
> I let him walk out the door after that, but I was very upset. I don't know what his problems are—and I feel so helpless. The whole experience has made me think that *Romeo and Juliet* is the last thing on a lot of these kids' minds—so many of them have such huge problems! What can I do to help? There was a substitute there that day, and it was obvious that she had been in a lot of classrooms—she was very comforting and told me we can't always be teacher and savior.

Even though there is much to say about these two slices, I want to focus here on how paying attention functions in the practice of these two teachers and how theory complicates the situations in which they find themselves as they respond to and try to make sense of—as they try to reflect on—their experiences with students who challenge them. My sense of it is that the teacher who wrote the first slice of life is operating from commitment to a strongly held, explicitly understood theory of ethnicity, curriculum, and the social responsibility of teachers. Her actions as a teacher are informed by the way she enacts the specific terms of the theory. Even though the position she takes is a solid and familiar one that she assumes everyone can easily understand, and even though she is practicing self-awareness and even self-criticism, there is little indication that she is paying attention to her student.

There are, on the other hand, indications that a perfectly good theory has been switched on, turned to full blast, and is drowning out what the student is saying. This slice of life is full of the teacher's own beliefs and makes only passing reference to the student. What the teacher does say about the student focuses on details, such as the "melting pot," which serve to identify the student as the holder of a counter-theory.

The language the teacher uses is heavy with terms that elaborate her theory, such as "ethnicity" and "polyethnic," or terms that suggest argument, such as "I validated my point" and "crucial topics." Argument, finally, is what theories often lead us to—whether we get them from someone else or make them up for ourselves out of our own reflections—and argument is often the form that arises when we arrive at theory, believe it, and stop paying attention. In some instances using theory to organize argument or argument to organize theory can be very useful in forming or revising teaching practice. But in this instance theory and argument seem to distract from what is happening with this student in the moment—a serious matter because this particular moment, and not its theoretical possibilities, may represent the best or only chance anyone will ever have to broaden a narrow mind long overdue for broadening.

What of the student teacher, then? In the first place, I do not think that she is acting on the basis of any recognizable theory. Indeed, she seems to be operating without any guidance whatsoever. She does display, however, a fair measure of savvy or street smarts, which arise, I would say, from her ability to reflect-in-action. After all, it may be a matter of no small importance that she was able to avoid violence in this volatile exchange. What is most interesting to me, though, is the highly attentive way this student teacher describes her actions and the earthy directness of her account. Her writing suggests that she is concentrating strongly on what her student says and how her student acts, picking up on body movement, expression, and tone of voice. She also seems deeply immersed in the action and aware of how the developing situation fits in the context of her lesson plan and the pattern and flow of the class. I do not think it is an accident that in the process of practicing concentration she ends up making significant adjustments in both the way she understands her student and in the way she understands the personal and professional roles and responsibilities of teachers.

These slices of life, plus thousands of others I have read, illustrate both the function of paying attention and the difficulty of doing so. Yet, at the heart of any serious practice—personal, professional, spiritual—lies not only attention but persistence. And, as I know only too well, failure. No matter how often they fail, though, serious practitioners return to the present point of practice, dig in, and press on—not stubbornly, not dogmatically, not angrily, but persistently. And openly. Always we should try to be open to our whole sense of what is happening around us and within us, to the continual flow of action, to the possibilities that arise in our practice, and even the possibility that sometimes the best way of proceeding is by retreating or withdrawing altogether. And if we are open, so often we find that the problem lies not so much outside ourselves with our students or the institutions within which we work, but within ourselves. If we can focus our attention and concentrate there, much can change for both our students and our institutions. Let me close this chapter with my own retelling of a classic Zen story.

One day a theorist and professor of English education, Professor Bob, decided to go visit Oryoki Roshi, the campus Zen Master, to see what he could learn. When Professor Bob arrived at the Zen Master's hut out behind the cattle barns (this was a land grant university), the Zen Master invited him in, seated him at a low table, and went to brew tea. When the tea was ready the Zen Master set the table with cups and saucers and salted peanuts (remember, this is my retelling of the story and I really like peanuts). Then the Zen Master proceeded to pour tea into Professor Bob's cup while Professor Bob sat there thinking about the book he was writing and what he would ask the Zen Master. When the tea reached the rim of Professor Bob's cup he still sat there thinking and the Zen Master kept pouring. Finally the tea spilled over into the saucer, overflowed from there onto the table, and then began to run into Professor Bob's lap. The hot tea in his lap brought Professor Bob back to attention and he jumped up, yelling, "Stop! Stop! My cup is full!"

And the Zen Master turned to him and said, "Yes, your cup is full, just as you are full of opinions and theories and your own self-importance. If there is anything you want from me, you will first of all have to empty your mind of what you think you know, and then you might be able to pay attention to what is happening and begin to learn."

Chapter Five

The Third Pillar:
Begin the Journey

Each journey, each person's journey, begins in its own unique place, and that is wherever the traveler is at the beginning. No two journeys, even journeys along the same route at the same time toward the same destination, begin in the same place. Even if a group of people start out together at the same moment on the same clearly defined journey, and they leave from the same clearly defined location, they start from different places. No matter how much there may be in common, each person brings to each beginning a different life history than anyone else, and leaves under different circumstances from a different point in life with different thoughts, different conditions and conditionings. Following is a poem of mine that is about a group of us—my cousins and I—leaving our hometown and driving together to a place called Mini-Wakan to fish for walleyes on the grade at Spirit Lake.

Your First Time Driving the Milford Blacktop

There isn't a bend in this road
all the way from 59
to Milford, not a ripple.
You could lay brick on the fence lines.

Most of what you see
the glaciers left,
O'Brien County like stained glass,
distant swelling,
groin deep black soil,
the sky is a green mist
near May City.

Night and cold water lie ahead.
Fish with eyes like mirrors
move out of your dreams,
bending their spines, ice
gone out of them at last,
waves breathing for them,
filling their clean jaws with light.

This is the other end of the line.
You can find your way here with no more
directions than these. Just be mindful.
Watch for stones collapsed like broken teeth
across the grade, the tightness of bark
about your legs and belly, your fingers
growing numb, disappearing,
feathers blowing across your palm.

Afterward, you will know everything
anyone knows about this road,
how close the sky is, how patient
the tireless curve beneath you,
how far the wind can travel
before it turns, building speed
at the corner of your eyes.

You will know at last
what it's like to drive both ways,
what big engines were made for,
whiskey and high beams,
and there won't be a star
in the north you haven't touched,
an animal of any shape
you haven't been. (1991, 9)

In one sense it is accurate to say that everyone in this story and poem was on the same fishing trip: we left from the same town, rode together in the same vehicle, waded in the same water, fished the same way, went back home together, and ate the same early morning meal of fresh, sweet walleye fillets. Not only that, but we were also members of the same extended family and closely related gene pool. If ever there were a shared, common experience, this was one. Yet I was the only one who experienced the trip in the particular way I did, who caught or did not catch the fish I did, who thought what I thought, felt as I felt, and wrote the poem I wrote. My fishing trip, my journey, was uniquely mine: even though I traveled with others, I traveled alone.

In the same sense, neither did all the fishermen begin in exactly the same place. This is how it is for teachers' journeys. It is true that most teachers begin in the same kinds of places, attending the same kinds of colleges and universities, taking the same kinds of courses, student teaching, getting first jobs, and so on. In these respects most teachers, like most other professionals, experience much in common. But just as each teacher's path touches on other teachers' paths, so do all paths diverge right from the beginning.

In the Bone

As my own story of confusion, indecision, and failure suggests, making a career choice by entering a teacher education program, and actually beginning to live the teaching life are not at all the same. The process is more complicated and indeterminate. For some teachers, the point of truly beginning the journey is clear and arises naturally, almost mysteriously. For others, finding the path with a heart can be the search of a lifetime. One teacher, Amanda, who has been teaching for more than thirty years and with whom I recently had a conversation, began her journey this way early in life:

> When I was a year-and-a-half or two years old and couldn't talk very well, I got this pointing stick and I got up and gave a lecture about this rocking horse that I had and I pointed to all its parts and I lectured to the whole family and they had to sit and listen. I didn't even have vocabulary yet, but I was going to be a teacher from the time I was born. There was never a question. The first thing I ever played was school. I was the teacher and anybody in the vicinity had to be a student. I was a real no-nonsense, awful disciplinarian with the ruler, the grade books. I made kids sit in little rows and do their stuff. I was just terrible, but . . . I knew always, that I would be a teacher. . . . It just felt like the natural thing.

> *Were your parents teachers?*

> No. My mother has a high school education. She never worked outside the home. My father taught for two years right before he retired. But most of his life he worked as a draftsman. . . . But I come from a family of teachers. My great aunts and uncles—my grandmother was a music teacher. My great-grandmother . . . [graduated from high school] at 16, got a college degree at 18, and taught music.

Diane, like Amanda, also describes such a natural beginning to her life as a teacher that it seems to have proceeded directly from the DNA inscribed in the cells of her body and the lessons she learned as a child.

> You know, I don't really think I thought about it too much in the beginning. Everybody in my family was a teacher. I liked English. I was always good at that and never really considered that I would be a

writer. I lived my life as a teacher. My father was a university professor. I was used to that teaching schedule. You know, the summers and
all that. Both my sisters are English teachers. My grandmother was a
teacher. My grandfather was a university professor. It was just in my
blood.

Family background, however powerful an influence, is unpredictable, though. It might help define a beginning to a teacher's journey,
and it might not. In my case, at first anyway, family background did not
seem to help much, and it certainly did not help one of my students,
Bill, whose family pushed him into teaching. I met Bill when he took
the first of two classes from me. In this class Bill was an indifferent student who claimed to be committed to teaching but who never seemed
to be fully engaged in his academic work. In fact, Bill was so less-than-
fully engaged that I had to give him a low grade, thus requiring him to
retake the class. That pattern of indifference continued throughout the
next semester when he took the second class from me, and even though
his performance the second time around improved considerably from
the first, I had many reservations when it came time for him to begin
student teaching.

Student teaching turned out to be an ordeal. Even though it was
possible for Bill to go through the motions on campus, he completely
broke down in student teaching. I have never seen a student teacher so
tight, so uncomfortable, so obviously out of place in the classroom. He
could not even come close to beginning to begin much less achieve beginning itself. Each time I tried to talk with him about his problems,
each time I asked him to explain what he was feeling, he became more
and more tied up and tongue-tied and unable to make contact with his
own experiences, feelings, and thoughts. This tightness grew and grew
until finally Bill became basically unable to stand up in front of his high
school students and conduct the simple routines of the classroom.

At that point Bill, no longer able to talk with his students, began
talking with me, and I was able to put parts of his story together so that
they made sense to me. His mother had been an elementary school
teacher who went on to become a principal. His father, too, was a former teacher who had moved into an administrative position. All his life
Bill's father had encouraged Bill to become a teacher until it got to the
point where he could not imagine himself doing anything else—despite the fact that there was nothing he could point to that he actually
liked about teaching. When the truth about his own feelings started
pressing in on him and he began to understand he was in the wrong
place, Bill became virtually paralyzed. All through this time, though,
his father continued pushing and trying to do Bill's thinking for him.
Trapped as he was, and unable to make any decisions on his own, Bill

finally came to a complete stop—and it was over—no matter what his father thought or did.

No one can find a beginning in someone else's life. All of us must find our own ways to live and our own beginnings, but wherever and however we find them we will discover that the solid ones are built on deep structures. In Ireland they say "What's bred in the bone will out," and that is where beginnings must be found. For Amanda and Diane it was easy and immediate. For me, it took a long time to find a beginning, and my first years in search of it were full of wrong turns and false starts, disorganized hopes and fears. Emily, who is in her fifth year of teaching, also wandered around some. When she found her beginning, though, it was bone deep and clear that she had arrived.

Emily came from a farming family. When she first went to the university, she majored in journalism with the intention of eventually working her way to Washington, D.C. Despite her advisor's suggestion that she wait to write for the university's newspaper until her sophomore year, Emily started right out in her first semester and was soon writing forty hours a week, getting bylines every day, in addition to getting A's in all her courses and holding down a part-time job. Despite her success, though, she realized early on that "something was missing." It started when she noticed that some of her teachers were not doing a very good job. In a conversation I had with her, she told me what she started thinking about her teachers:

> "They're terrible. I could do that better." I'm not kidding you. I remember sitting in class one day thinking that "this is so wrong the way they're doing that. I could do that better." And as much as I enjoyed the writing there was something missing. I didn't get the feeling that what I was doing was helping anybody. It was all for me. Front page bylines. The excitement. And I loved all that.

As time went on and she got into the second semester of her first year, the feeling that something was missing continued with the growing realization that the pressure to "get the story" was forcing her into what she considered unethical and "cutthroat" practices. And then one day, seemingly out of nowhere, she had a remarkable experience that ended her life as a journalist and served as the beginning of her journey as a teacher.

> I went to church one day and the priest was talking about choosing a career where you would serve God and the people around you and not yourself. And right there. I can remember where I was sitting. I can remember who I was sitting by. And I thought, "I'm in the wrong career."

> *My god!*

And I walked out. I went to my advisor on Monday morning and I said to her, "I'm changing my major," and she looked at me and said, "You what?"

Holy cow. You were struck blind on the road to Damascus!

I really was. It was incredible. And my advisor started crying in her office. She said, "You're the best freshman we've ever had in this program." She got the head of the department to come in. He offered me money. It was the toughest thing I'd ever done up to that point in my life. I can remember walking out and not having one question. Not one. I never looked back.

Need to Serve

Besides illustrating the importance of "in the bone" there are two additional points I want to emphasize in Emily's account of her beginning. The first is that her decision in church to follow the path with a heart really did not come out of nowhere. Although it seems like Emily literally walked in the door of the church as a star journalism student and walked out a teacher, her ability to pay attention to her own teachers and her reactions to them laid the groundwork for conversion despite the heady, distracting rush she got from journalism. Not only did she know that "something was missing" in her life and her classes, she knew instinctively something very important about herself: she knew that she could do better.

Stories like hers make me wonder how often similar possibilities present themselves to us and we dismiss them because we do not know ourselves well enough to know what we really want or need. How often have how many of us failed to take ourselves seriously because we were either not paying attention or just plain afraid? Afraid of change? Afraid of the truth? Afraid of family? Afraid of ourselves? The voice in the cornfield says, "If you build it, he will come." The voice crying in the desert says, "Make ready the way." The voices inside ourselves say . . . what? And who is listening?

The second point I want to emphasize in Emily's story is that as a journalist, cutthroat Emily served herself. She did not find her real beginning place until she realized the need she had to move out beyond herself. Hearing her talk about God was an unusual experience for me. For many reasons, some good, some not so good, God is not a topic that comes up very often in conversations I have with teachers. What is common, though, is to hear teachers talk about the desire they have, the need they feel, to serve others, to make positive differences in other people's lives. This need, wherever it comes from, can be a powerful source in leading to beginning. Diane, at one point in the conversation I had with her, said,

> [Teaching] was always what I was going to do. And I think I stayed with it—through some pretty rough times—sometimes overwhelming—because I think it's a noble thing to do. I don't think I can do something where I don't feel like I'm making a contribution. I need that. I need to feel like when I go to work each day I'm not just doing some kind of menial job. That I'm affecting society somehow. And so, even sometimes when I get discouraged, I come back to that. I make a difference somehow.

In the case of the following teacher, Frank, it was not until he had been teaching for fifteen years that discovering the need to serve caused him to truly find his beginning as a teacher. Frank started teaching in the early seventies in a small town. His job involved teaching courses in history and social studies as well as coaching football and wrestling. Toward the end of his five-year tenure in that job, he began and completed a master's degree in counseling and immediately took a job in a larger district, where he continued coaching football and designed and taught a course in family living. He worked in that schedule for ten years until his school, like many other schools at the time, established a program for at-risk students. Despite serious misgivings, Frank, along with another teacher, accepted an appointment to direct the "resource center."

Being transferred to the resource center changed Frank's professional life. He admits that in the fifteen years leading up to that point, he had become mired in a narrow and mechanical view of teaching practice:

> I'll be honest with you—before I worked with at-risk kids I was not half the teacher that I am today. I mean, I just didn't get it. I did the same stuff year after year, and I just got through the day in the sense that I didn't choose a curriculum and I didn't sit down and plan. Now, I'd been taught all those things in my methods courses. My theory is that for most of us, what happens is that those first two years we're so worried about keeping our heads above water that curriculum is not important. So, when I first started teaching American history I didn't think things like, "what am I going to teach, am I going to get through the book, how fast do I have to go?" I thought, "Jesus, how am I going to do this?" So, what happened was I picked something and taught it, and if it worked I did it the next year. And before long I developed a curriculum, but it was a real haphazard way to do it, and I taught the way I had been taught.

Which was?

Lecture method. "OK kids, here's the stuff on the board. This is the stuff you've got to remember. Du-dah-du-dah-du-dah. Five days in a row and we take a test on the sixth day." I always learned well that way. It came easy to me and I didn't try to be creative. So I did that for five years in my first job, and I think I did pretty much the same thing for ten years here.

In the resource center Frank discovered that what he could take for granted in the classroom he could no longer take for granted. One of his first realizations, for example, was that in his teaching practice up to that point he had been ignoring or writing off students who frustrated him. In the resource center, where all his students were frustrating in one way or other, Frank had to completely redefine his fifteen-year relationship with students, with frustration, and, inevitably, with himself. At another point in our conversation he said:

> You know, it's real easy when you face 150 kids a day to get to the point where you feel like the kid who doesn't do his work is your enemy. And working with at-risk kids taught me that they're anything but my enemy. These are kids who want to please. But they've been frustrated for one reason or another, personal life, school life, whatever it might be. And it's my job to try to figure out how to get them interested. Sometimes I figure it out and most of the time I don't. But the thing that makes me different now is that I try.

Learning that the students in the resource center needed him in a way that students never had before, learning that he needed to "try," learning the need to "serve," I would say, marked the true beginning of Frank's teaching life. He discovered in the resource center what Emily discovered sitting in church, that "teachers become teachers because they want to help people." Here, in another excerpt from my conversation with Frank, he describes his view of this need to serve:

> I believe teachers become teachers because they want to help people. Obviously we don't do this for the money. Most people are motivated by the right thing. There are some who want to become teachers because they don't think it's real hard work. And for them it never will be.

Ha-ha. That's right.

> But most people want to teach because they see that possibly they can positively affect other people. What I learned in the resource center was that if you take kids like that a little further, give them a little bit extra, it can really pay off. It's not a question of intelligence. In fact a lot of disaffected kids are above average intelligence—as you already know. So it's not that. It's finding the direction, it's finding the place to come in from.

Obviously, unlike Emily, for Frank this need to serve was not a dominating factor in his early decision to teach. The first few years of Frank's life as a teacher, as he describes them anyway, seem quite self-centered.

Early on, like all beginning teachers, he was mainly concerned with survival. Later on it was coaching and winning that defined his interest, not work in the classroom and not the needs of individual students. The lecture-recitation-test pattern of practice he describes is by definition a self-centered way of practice that reduces, sometimes to a bare minimum, the amount of contact a teacher has with students. While that might be an effective way to accomplish certain specific goals, as a dominant practice it leaves much to be desired.

However, for Frank this kind of teacher-centered practice did not turn out to be the practice that dominated his teaching life. In a manner more gradual but no less stunning or dramatic than Emily's, Frank enters the resource center, "wake[s] up one day" and becomes a whole new teacher and person, more aware of himself, his students, and everyone's needs. Why did it take him fifteen years? I do not know for sure. Was it that he simply had not been exposed to what he finally came to understand? Apparently not. He indicated that he had heard the wake-up call as early as his college days and methods classes. Why did he not heed it then? Perhaps he was not ready. Perhaps he was not ready because he was unable to break loose from the comfortable, familiar pattern he remembered from his own schooling. After all, if it was good enough for his teachers and if he "always learned well that way," why should he pay any attention to some pointy-headed methods teacher spouting crazy ideas that seemed to have nothing at all to do with first-and-ten and the Real World?

Perhaps fifteen years is not such a long time. The beginning does not always lie in the beginning, and if it took Frank fifteen years to discover the need he had to serve, then it was fifteen years well spent. Sometimes the teacher we become lies beyond the teacher whose life we thought we were living. And sometimes, when we discover who the teacher we will become is, what we learn is that we are already living in that teacher's home and did not really know it.

Ironically, and humorously too, when Frank's real teaching life began, the part that ended up dying off was the part that constituted his main interest early on: coaching football.

What ever became of the coaching, then?

I'm ashamed to say that after seventeen years it got to the point where I started slipping into one of those areas I didn't want to be in. Winning became more important than teaching the sport. Winning the game became more important than teaching all of the benefits of the sport. It felt to me that I cared more about winning than the kids did. So I just backed off.

Was that kind of a gradual understanding that you came to?

It was real gradual, but there was a defining moment. . . . The last game
that we played in the last year that I coached, two of my starters—this
is more about them than it is me—two of my starters left their helmets
at home.

Ha-ha. Oh god!

And they'd started all year. How can you do that? Ha-ha. . . . So I
just stopped and thought, "You know what? I think I'd like to just
teach." So I did and I'm having more fun now than I've ever had in
my life.

Beyond Pattern

Frank's story brings up the question of where beginnings fit in the pattern of a whole teaching life. Oftentimes new teachers entering the profession feel as if there is some set, linear pattern of development all
teachers must follow from day one. Occasionally students of mine have
become upset when their progress did not conform to the ideal pattern
they had imagined for themselves. To think along such lines may be
common, but Frank's story suggests that even a matter so seemingly
simple as "beginning" can be highly ambiguous and unpredictable. Entering a teacher education program, taking methods classes, and then
proceeding onward through the familiar sequence of professional development has nothing to do with what is really going on or what will
happen next.

Trying to predict a beginning point and any kind of pattern for any
life is an enterprise that will fail more times than it will succeed. For me
it makes sense to balance all ideas of pattern and predictability with a
return to my earlier mantra, "Each day is just each day." Once I heard
an old Kansas quail hunter, who was used to the patterned behavior of
that species, scoff at the mere mention of pheasants. "The only thing
predictable about a pheasant is its unpredictability," he said. "They'll
run when they should fly, fly when they should run, and sit tight in a
scrap of cover you wouldn't think would hide a mouse." Likewise, living the teacher's life on any particular day at any particular age can
contain surprises within surprises, paradoxes within paradoxes. Sometimes we can predict patterns that capture the shape of experience exactly; sometimes everything we thought was true disappears before our
very eyes as if it had feathers, a long tail, and flushed wild out of a blade
of grass one hundred yards downwind.

Following is part of a letter I once received from a student in which
he outlined his reasons for leaving the teacher education program for a
different major and career path. He surprised me as much as Emily must

have surprised her advisor. At the same time he provided me with a powerful lesson on the nature of beginnings and the limitations of thinking in terms of patterns:

> [This] wasn't something I decided on a whim over my second bowl of Frosted Flakes; it was a drawn out, even agonizing process of self-examination and questioning about my future. Was I really ready to be a teacher? The bottom line is this: I love literature and I'm a good writer—sometimes a damn good writer. The question was how college could help manifest that part of me in some way in order that I could live from it. I didn't get a holy vision of myself as a teacher when I was 5 or anything; "teacher" just seemed like a viable way to talk about books all day and make a living. . . . So I declared myself an English Education major, applied to the college of ed., and registered for Foundations of Education.
>
> I was never maniacally devoted to the idea or the path, and my doubts led me to contemplate changing my major at least twice a day. But I began to tell myself a new story about myself—that maybe I would be good and content as a teacher, that was really how I wanted to use my talent, etc. So the idea got incorporated into my little story and I stuck with it all the way to methods. The way I put that it sounds like methods was "the straw that broke . . ." But it wasn't. It was just a grinding semester overall, and the first semester in which I did an in-class observation, designed units, and lingered for more than fifty minutes in the educational atmosphere of the university itself. Something about that whole experience, along with a lot of reflection regarding the expectations I have for myself and the directions of my life as husband and father, helped make a decision for me. I wasn't ready to maniacally devote myself to an appreciation-lacking, life-endangering, 24-hour a day teaching job.
>
> I can't isolate any one of those factors and say that I couldn't deal with them. Somehow it's the conglomeration of them all which seems more overwhelming than satisfying. Maybe one year away from the bubbly world of academics will be enough to reconfigure my vision of what is "satisfying" and what's not, but right now I need to leave. I may be back, and if I do return it will be for real and for the gold.

This student reminded me that some beginnings should never begin. Teaching English, as I have said, is not just for anyone who "loves literature" or who is good at working with young people. Instead, teaching is for those who are willing to pay the price of commitment. At the simplest level, this means the commitment of time. This student, unlike many students, already knows that the teacher's work schedule is not limited to the daily and yearly school schedules spelled out in a contract. At a more complex level this means a commitment of self. This student, also unlike many students, is aware that professional life and personal life are, even at the beginning, close to being one life, and that everyone must find a way to live. This is an amazing insight for someone so inexperienced. Such an awareness does not come easily to most of us, and for that reason I was sorry to see him leave teacher education. When he left, he already knew—or at least sensed—so much that would have helped him find a solid beginning as a teacher. I was particularly glad, though, that he was willing to leave open the possibility of returning. People do return to begin; patterns do unpattern and turn back on themselves.

Once, a few years ago, I was sitting in my office when a woman appeared at my door. She was medium height with black hair and dark skin. I do not remember exactly what she was wearing, but I do remember a general impression of the color red and some kind of head covering that came down on her forehead. Her face was almost obscured by dark sunglasses with large lenses that covered a good portion of her face. Her appearance made me feel like a seedy, B-rated private eye—Guy Noir maybe—sitting in his office late at night in a city that never sleeps, when all of a sudden the beautiful, mysterious woman shows up.

The mysterious woman in this case turned out to be a woman who had graduated in English with honors about ten years before, and who had been working her way up a career ladder at a prominent local business ever since. As time passed she had come to feel, as Emily had felt from the beginning, that something was missing from her life. Finally, after much deliberation, she had decided that teaching was what she really wanted to do. Her appearance at my door—in disguise so as to escape the notice of employees from the business who were also students—was her way of beginning after having already been journeying a long time.

I like to think this mystery story had a happy ending. Soon after seeing me, the woman quit her job and came back to school full time. Because of her maturity, strength of purpose, and experience—to say nothing of her intelligence and academic expertise—she moved quickly and efficiently through the courses she needed, served as a student teacher with a great deal of success, got a job in a nearby high school, and won the "Best New Teacher" award at the end of her first year. Right now I do not know where she is for sure or if she is still teaching, but her story gives me hope that my good student who left teacher education might return someday if that is what he wants and if that is where his bones and blood lead him. Her story also gives me hope that even if other beginnings for other teachers are delayed or interrupted they might yet be begun. Finally, her story convinces me that when it comes to formulating patterns or predicting the shape of a teaching life, overformulating or overpredicting will lead to frustration and disappointment. The cover and undergrowth in a teacher's life is crowded with pheasants, which are as capable of flushing up between your legs and into your face when you least expect it as they are of anything else.

Occasions to Begin

When I was young and taking Saturday morning religion classes, I remember my teachers talking about the "occasions of sin." What they meant by this term, which seemed strange to me at the time, had to do with temptation or tempting situations that should be treated with caution or avoided altogether lest they pull one into evil and wrongdoing. At first, I think I considered these occasions to be vague, threatening people or places that would, in some indefinable way, lure me off the path to righteousness I thought I was following at the time. As I got older, these occasions took on a much more concrete character, generally connected in some way with beer, sex, and cars. At some further point, about the time I would say my life started to become interesting, "occasions" became "opportunities" or "fun times," and then I stopped thinking about these concepts for quite a few years.

Lately I have begun thinking about them again, although in a more general way than before. The idea of "occasion" points to a globally valid concept not limited to religious education. All humans everywhere, every day, encounter a wide range of situations that, depending on how they are engaged, might be occasions that lead them to all sorts of results. Some of them, it is true, might be occasions of sin. But it is just as likely that any one of us at any given time might enter into an occasion that cuts the other way—an occasion that is a true opportunity. Occasions to begin the life of the teacher can pop up anywhere as easily as a child can pick up a pointing stick and start lecturing about a rocking horse. Teacher education programs have built within them certain broadly configured occasions that, in a formal way, are designed to function as opportunities to begin. These can, as they did for Frank and me, function as mere occasions to start a job rather than truly begin. Yet, they can also succeed in their design if the program they are part of is solid and the student is ready. In the following two sections I want to examine two of these occasions, methods courses and student teaching, and try to show some ways in which they may or may not lead to beginning.

Methods Courses: Begin to Question

I have mixed feelings about the usefulness and effectiveness of methods courses and the potential they hold to really provide students with solid occasions to begin. Of the varieties of methods courses out there, the kind that seems to me most likely to help in this way is the kind that has built within it actual field experience in schools. Schools, after all, are the places where most teachers become teachers and where beginning seems most likely to be occasioned. Unfortunately, in Smagorinsky and Whiting's research, which I summarized in Chapter 2, a relatively small number of such courses turned up. This is not to say that there are not many opportunities in many programs for various kinds of practicums and field experiences, but methods courses on the whole seem to ignore the potential here. Consequently, many methods students I have talked with have complained in varying degrees of moaning, groaning, and whining about the unreal quality of methods courses and believe that the approaches we ivory-tower academics take on campus are at best unrealistic or idealistic and at worst totally deluded. Many students believe that whatever journey they might begin in a methods class could lead them nowhere but to a classroom somewhere between Never-Never Land and the Kingdom of Oz.

To be honest, I share many of these perceptions and have many reservations about the value of methods courses, mine included. I even have reservations about those courses that do contain a field experience component: as in the case of the blind men and the elephant, it is sometimes just as easy to be deluded by limited hands-on experience as it is to be enlightened by it. My reservations have led me over the last several years to try to be honest with myself, if not my students, when thinking about the methods class. There are three primary ways in which a good, or even a mediocre, methods class can help students find a beginning for the journey. First, such a course can create the occasion to learn the basic principles, skills, and beliefs on which professional practice is based. Methods classes, after all, are about methods, materials, curriculums, theories, and so on that language arts professionals work with and from. Methods classes also are about the various political and ideological positions that characterize professional thinking and action. English teachers and organizations of English teachers like the National Council of Teachers of English and its state affiliates have much to say about matters such as multicultural education, censorship, grammar, dialect, and the role of the teacher and the school in culture and society. Sometimes we speak with one voice on such issues, and sometimes there is significant disagreement, but in order to begin the journey a teacher needs to understand the conversation of the other journeyers.

Second, a methods class can provide an occasion to begin thinking like a teacher—and to begin to stop thinking like a student. This is a hard but necessary transition to make. The first step is to recognize that the way every student thinks about teaching is to some extent controlled by patterns and habits of mind born of being a student. This is common sense. If you do something long enough, you begin to develop the mind that makes it possible to succeed at whatever you do. If you drive a truck long enough, for example, you habitually start thinking like a truck driver—and you keep thinking like a truck driver. Even after all these years, when an eighteen-wheeler passes me, without thinking about it, I flash my headlights so that the driver knows the trailer has cleared my vehicle and that it is safe to pull back out of what professionals call the "hammer lane." Likewise, students who have been students a long time think with students' minds, and even though this has gotten them to where they are, if they are not able to begin to lay their mental habits aside in methods class, there will be problems further up the road. Take the following vignette, for example, which I have borrowed from Ruth Vinz's (1996) classroom research on teaching. The scene features three players involved in a complicated student mind game and power struggle of the sort that goes on every day in the schools. Regina Riggs is a student teacher who has somehow passed out of methods class still thinking like a student and who consequently gets sucked right into a situation that she would be better off outgrowing and rising above. Ms. Murphy is her cooperating teacher, and Eugene is a high school student who should be the only one serious about playing games.

> Eugene has been sitting with blank paper in front of him [during a free writing exercise]. He's tapping his pencil on the side of his desk. Regina walks over to him, "Why aren't you writing?"
>
> "It's stupid," Eugene blurts out.
>
> "OK, well, just give it a try—you'll never know what you'll come up with." Ms. Riggs turns to talk with Martha who sits in front of Eugene.
>
> Eugene clenches his fists and swipes the paper on his desk onto the floor: "This is so stupid. This is ridiculous! Who's going to read this shit? Nobody will ever read it! This is not writing."
>
> "Eugene, I'm just asking that you try this. If it doesn't work for you, that's fine. You know that you can always work on your own writing for the rest of the period. I'm just asking that you give this a shot."
>
> "We've done this before! We keep doing it over and over again. It's just so stupid! No one's ever going to read this. What's the point?" Eugene pushes his notebook onto the floor. It falls with a loud thump. Joseph is suppressing giggles and Nick does too, until they see Regina glaring at them.
>
> "The reason why we're doing this, Eugene, is to develop your writing, to make it easier for you to brainstorm through your writing. All writers need to keep their skills sharp. Eugene, you have a right to express your opinion but not to disrupt the class. Just do it." Regina walks away.

> Eugene picks up the papers that have scattered across the floor.
> He stomps out of the room. (266)

It was exactly on such fields of battle that most of us in teacher education gained and then habituated our ability to think like students. Not all of us were Eugenes, though. Most likely we were versions of Joseph and Nick, two guys who are aware of what their place is and skillful at playing the game that Regina is unfortunately still caught up in. All that has changed for her is that, as a student teacher, she is learning a new position.

Otherwise, she is in exactly the same place Eugene is, and exactly the same place, too, as the college teacher whose slice of life I discussed at the end of the last chapter. Stuck as they are, all three of these people's actions narrow down to the same crude and primitive efforts to impose their wills on other people without ever bothering to pay attention to either those other people or the nature of the situations in which they find themselves. As much as anything else, this is a problem of attention. However, Regina is not close to recognizing this. On the contrary, the language she uses in describing her view of the matter is the language of political struggle and warfare.

> What would happen if all students did their own thing? I get frustrated with direct confrontations like this. I don't think students have the right to be so argumentative and just walk out of class. I think, on one hand, I need to do something to acknowledge that he did wrong, but, on the other hand, I want to have a truce.

To make the situation even more complex, Ruth Vinz is convinced that Ms. Murphy, the cooperating teacher, is also stuck in the same old student mind game and power struggle. Vinz writes:

> Regina's cooperating teacher, Ms. Murphy, suggested that there is "always a contest between your authority as a teacher and the students' need for power. One of the tricks I've learned is to make small concessions in order to protect my power when I need it." The view of authority relationships between teacher and pupils on a common sense level points to both Regina and Ms. Murphy's beliefs that they need to maintain control over students. Their prescribed construct of power leads to practices that perpetuate teacher control.

Regina is in two binds here. First, despite having progressed most of the way through a teacher education program, she still thinks pretty much like her students and has the same kinds of expectations when it comes to interactions and conflicts in the classroom. So, apparently, does Ms. Murphy. This is a game played by three generations of minds that work in the same way, all thinking like students. Who will win? Will the teacher use her power to force the students into her way of thinking and acting? Or will the students outfox, outface, or outwit the teacher? Before Regina or other education students can really begin the journey they must find ways of answering these questions. Even more important, they need to find ways of answering a bigger question: is it possible to cultivate a teacher's mind, a way of thinking and acting, that does not have to get bogged down in such games and questions in the first place? Is it possible to cultivate such a mind in the institution of the school as it exists today? Is it possible to do so while operating simultaneously in the role of student and teacher? If you wait to work on such questions until you are student teaching, you have waited too long. Methods class, on the other hand, can create a powerful occasion to begin. Working on such questions, even if no answers are forthcoming, is a beginning in itself because these are questions worthy of building a whole teaching life on.

A second bind Regina is in is that Ms. Murphy, the cooperating teacher, and Ruth Vinz, the English education professor, have different views about the kind of teacher's mind Regina should cultivate. Ms. Murphy is professionally committed to power and mind games and is certain that Regina must learn how "to maintain control over students." Ms. Murphy, despite her years of experience, has not seen any reason to move beyond the "common sense" reward-and-punishment-based habits of mind she cultivated as a student, held on to through methods class, and adapted to her practice as a teacher. Nor is she entirely wrong in her perceptions and practice given the current system. She knows that failing to maintain order means failing to keep your job. No matter what else Regina does, if she wants to survive, she has to play the game and win. Period. Vinz, for her part, does not want Regina just to survive, but also, as she says, to "interrogate fully and carefully where control and power reside in a discourse on schools" (267). Vinz believes that there is something deeply amiss in the way the institution of the school is organized and run. She knows that lessons have been missed, and she wants Regina and other beginning teachers to make a difference by looking for ways to change the traditional ways of thinking that Ms. Murphy represents. What is Regina to do, caught as she is between two powerful and opposing forces?

The short answer, as I said, is that Regina must survive. That, after all, is the First Pillar. The fuller answer, though, is not so easy, and leads me into the third way a methods class might provide an occasion to begin: the methods class can make clear and help students attend to the fact that there are at least two agendas operating in the profession today and that situations like the one that Regina found herself in offer real opportunities for understanding the processes of progress and reform. The first agenda is Ms. Murphy's agenda for living and thinking in the institution. The second agenda is embodied in the image of the interrogating mind that Ruth Vinz brings to her discussion of Regina's situation. Vinz's agenda is an activist one that seeks to encourage—or in its strongest manifestations push—education students, right from the start, not only to begin thinking like teachers, but to begin thinking beyond the kind of mind that Ms. Murphy brings to her practice. English educators and methods teachers do not just want our students to become teachers; we want them to become teachers who will work to reform the way schools and language arts classes are run. Methods class is where we start working to create occasions for beginning teachers to begin changing their minds.

Joy Ritchie and David Wilson use the term "behaviorist" to describe Ms. Murphy's mind and agenda, and "transformative" to describe Vinz's and other English educators' agenda for changing minds and reforming schools. The idea behind transformative thinking and teaching is that if students coming out of methods classes can be convinced to begin adopting a nonconfrontational, cooperative, student-centered approach to practice, one that is not limited to gaining power and control over students, then schools will become different kinds of institutions where students and teachers will share the effort and responsibility for learning. This is a wonderful vision, that is at the heart of the century-long progressive reform movement, but it is a hard sell when it comes to teachers like Ms. Murphy and the traditional kind of school she works in. Oftentimes the result is nothing more than an additional layer of conflict for education students. Here is how Ritchie and Wilson lay it out:

> We had hoped that upon completion [our students] would have experienced and subsequently developed an understanding of reading, writing, and language learning as complicated personal and dialogic processes. We had hoped that they would develop an understanding of themselves as teachers/learners and of the importance of their students becoming their own teachers. And finally we had hoped that they would develop a constructivist vision of education—of the philosophical, ethical, and political purposes of education—consistent with the above understandings. (1993, 67)

What Ritchie and Wilson learn, though, is that they are up against a deeply-embedded system:

> We were taught that there is another [way of thinking] that plays a much more important role in determining our pre-service teachers' . . . understanding of themselves as teachers and their visions of education [than the one we are trying to teach them in methods classes]. This other [understanding] extends from pre-school to young adulthood and thus is more pervasive and powerful, involving almost every class these students have taken, and almost every teacher with whom they have interacted. Their experience of a few Teachers

College and English Department courses does *not* shape their under-standings. Instead, it is their experience as students . . . in a behaviorist educational system—a system which views the teacher as the author-ity figure and knower, a system which views writing and reading as "skills," reducing the complexity and creativity of language learning—that determines who these students believe themselves to be and what they do as teachers. (68)

Regina's bind is the bind that ties us all together. It can be tight. If the education student does not follow the agenda that is set in the uni-versity methods course, the result could be a huge ration of grief, a bad grade, a lousy recommendation, and no beginning. On the other hand, if the student ends up working in a traditional school with a teacher like Ms. Murphy, the result could be equally disastrous. The bind gets even tighter when we recognize the fact that both sides are correct. The transformativists are correct that there are severe limitations in the way schools operate and teachers and students think and relate to each other. The Ms. Murphys are also right, though. If beginning teachers want to survive long enough in the schools to do anything, they had bet-ter learn to win the mind games, get down in the mud and fight, and hold the power. The power struggle is going on at many levels and in-volves numerous matchups: poor Regina must play the power game with Eugene in the role of teacher, but she must also play it out as a stu-dent when she interacts with her professors or Ms. Murphy. No one is evil here, no one wants anything but the best, but everyone does want his or her own way.

This has all the features of a classic catch-22. In order to become a good teacher and transform and reform the schools, beginners must approach practice with a new and transformed kind of mind that is dif-ferent from the controlling, behaviorist mind they grew up with as stu-dents. But in order to survive long enough to make even one measly transformation or reformation, the beginner must learn to think and act well enough with the old kind of mind to be able to survive in the school where she or he begins teaching. This catch-22 helps show why Vinz's commentary on Regina and Ms. Murphy's problem is so sage. Vinz does not say that Regina should do such-and-such and that Ms. Murphy should do so-and-so. Instead, she wants nothing more—or less—than for Regina to have an occasion, as I mentioned, "to probe more deeply into issues of power relations and how those might be examined," and "to interrogate fully and carefully where power and control reside" (267). This may not seem like much, but, just by itself, it defines exactly a main field of action and a major objective for students in methods courses—regardless of what the actual course content may be—and a ripe occasion to begin a teaching life there. That, and not later, is the time to start asking questions, asking hard questions, thinking, beginning to think for yourself, beginning to think like a teacher.

However, as Larry Cuban (1993) concluded in his study of one hundred years of school reform, these processes of habit, power, control, and transformation have been unfolding for a long time, have evolved slowly, and are likely to continue unfolding and evolving for a much longer time. Since the late 1800s, Cuban says, not much has fundamentally changed in the way most classrooms are run. Ms. Murphy and the kind of thinking she represents is still very much present and largely unexamined in most schools. So Regina, Vinz, Ritchie, Wilson, and the rest of us had better start right away preparing for a lengthy campaign and be willing to make the journey our home because we are going to be on it a long time. What we do and the effort we put forth will make a difference, though, even if it is hard to see. As Dogen wrote, "running water, no matter how little, can eventually wear away rock" (Yokoi 1990, 176).

Student Teaching: Begin to Live with Uncertainty

What student teaching is and how you should approach it depends on who you talk to and when you talk to them. For example, when I asked my wife, Michelle, who has taught middle school and high school for twenty years and who has worked with many student teachers, what particular occasion to begin student teaching holds, she responded by saying that student teaching can give us the opportunity to "try on the clothing" of a teacher. The terms of this metaphor depict student teaching as a period of experimentation that can create an occasion for us to work with the outfits we've carried with us from campus and to negotiate the fit and appropriateness of our dress with the wardrobe of the school and our cooperating teacher.

I have at best a crude and rudimentary concept of dress and wardrobe, but there is something in this metaphor that works for me. For one thing, student teaching, like a change of clothes, is a temporary, provisional situation that may bear any range of possible relationships to whatever teacher's life we have waiting for us beyond it. In many ways student teaching has a superficial, even unreal, feel to it since it is so short-lived, so closely bound in time and space, and occurs in someone else's school and classroom where our role—guest, apprentice, or fully invested professional—is not always clear. When we enter student teaching—unless there is a strict dress code enforced by a controlling cooperating teacher—we often do, I think, try on garments of various kinds, wear them, change them often or infrequently, and then, when we leave, put whatever gown, suit, or set of rags we have ended up with away, put on our traveling clothes, and move on. The way we look when we leave may be similar to the way we looked when we arrived or we might be so changed that we barely recognize ourselves. The only sure thing is that we do not want to leave naked or covered in ashes or arrayed in tar and feathers and riding a rail out of town.

Even though this metaphor works for a couple of veteran teachers like Michelle and me, it does not always work very well for my students. They are able to see that student teaching has a transitory, superficial nature about it, but they are uncertain about that and often much more aware of its deadly serious side. The reason for this is that when we come to student teaching we have traveled a long way—if not in terms of miles at least in terms of time and effort. There is a lot riding on what happens in student teaching. It is easy to believe that if it does not go well, our academic careers and all the time and money we have invested will be lost. Thus, for many of us early in our careers, student teaching seems as much like a final barrier or invisible gate that we must somehow get through unharmed as it does a style show.

The truth is that there *is* a lot at stake in student teaching, but also that there is no one way to regard it or predict what it will be like. Thus, I believe that the key to finding an occasion to begin in student teaching depends on the way each student teacher approaches this fundamental uncertainty and begins shaping the teaching life that lies on the other side.

For, example, add to Regina's catch-22 the situation John faces in the following vignette, which I have also drawn from Ruth Vinz. When we pick up the action, John is struggling with his cooperating teacher, Mr. McMurtrey, who is a man with unambiguous opinions about what a student teacher should do and how. In this first excerpt John writes that

> Mr. McMurtrey prefers a more structured and detailed approach. His points follow one another logically, and his questions are information oriented. "Where did Huck and Jim flee to?" He insists upon detailed lesson plans and lists of unit goals in advance. As I tried to fit my techniques with his methods, my spontaneity decreased and student discussion tailed off. He made suggestions to stimulate student participation (some quite valuable), but we never really got it back. It seemed like the more informational and teacher oriented the class was, the more he liked it. I was not allowed to read to the students just for fun, nor could I let them read anything in class. "Pleasure reading is extra-curricular and homework is done exactly where the word says—at home." I'm sure he enjoys literature, but it seemed that much of his method turned the course into work. Work, of course, is not to be shunned, but if delight is expelled from literature, it becomes drudgery. And little, I feel, is learned from drudgery. (1996, 260)

Clearly, John is not happy with Mr. McMurtrey's approach to teaching, his structured requirements for planning, or his work ethic for students. It is hard to say here whether Mr. McMurtrey is being harsh and unreasonable with everyone—as John seems to believe—or if John has an uninformed sense about what should go on in the classroom and why. For his part, though, here is what Mr. McMurtrey has to say:

> Well, I know that John wants, or thinks he wants, the students to think for themselves, so he's pretty loose with the kinds of questions he asks. I see kids getting confused, not really knowing what's going on or why. That isn't helpful to them. They get way off track and have trouble understanding why they are discussing at all. John's open-minded and takes every answer as equal. I think that if one of the students said that Huck is really an alien from outer space, John would pursue the interpretation. I mean there's a limit. He calls it open-minded. I call it silly. (261)

Like Regina, John is in a real bind here that must seem very confusing to him. According to the progressive, student-centered agenda he seems to have carried with him from his methods courses, John feels he is doing everything right. He is giving his students opportunities to respond to and interpret texts, he is trying to motivate his students by making reading pleasurable, he is allowing ample time in class for student talk and student writing. His approach, in the terms used by Ritchie and Wilson, is "constructivist," "dialogic," "personal," and decidedly "transformative." John, according to his own account, could be a poster boy for Ritchie and Wilson and the rest of us in English Education who are committed to reform. He has found a beginning in methods class and is all geared up and ready to go out and change the world. What he is not ready for, though, is Mr. McMurtrey. Mr. McMurtrey, at least in John's eyes, could be the poster boy for Ritchie and Wilson's "behaviorist" or "reductionist" teacher. His agenda, according to John, is a control agenda, teacher-centered and authoritarian. Also, according to John, Mr. McMurtrey does not seem to care half so much what his students think as he cares that they get their homework done at home and stick to business in class.

Unfortunately, the conflict between John and Mr. McMurtrey only makes sense if we raise it to this fairly high level of abstraction, give the participants labels, and argue it out theoretically and ideologically. When we get right down to it, though, student teaching is not like the discussions of theory and ideology, transformationalism and behaviorism that we might have in a methods class. The questioning, probing, and interrogating that serves as an occasion to begin in that setting must be taken on the road. In contrast to the home field comfort of methods, student teaching is a full contact away game in which intellectual clarity, rational thought, and the meaning of abstract labels easily get lost in a sometimes brutal and chaotic clash of wills and egos. The following commentary from Vinz shows what happens when the rational constructs of educational theory get pulled through the irrational guts of real people. The scene is a meeting of John, McMurtrey, and Vinz. McMurtrey is the first speaker:

> "Some of the students are coming to me and saying they're losing respect for you, that you don't make them behave, that you don't seem to be teaching them anything about literature. . . ."
>
> "Well, nobody's going to please everybody, so I can't worry too much about it." John juts out his chin and repositions his body so that he leans further away from Mr. McMurtrey.
>
> Mr. McMurtrey pursues the idea, "What do you mean, you can't worry about it?"
>
> "I mean that I accept the fact that not everybody is going to like me." John begins to put his books and papers in his briefcase as if getting ready to end the conversation.
>
> "Five students have talked to me in private about you and they don't like . . ."
>
> "Two can play that game! You want to hear what students say to me about you? Nobody's universally popular. Not you. Not me. Nobody."
>
> "So now you're attacking me? You're the guest in this classroom." Mr. McMurtrey slams his hand on the table.
>
> "Guest. Guest? I thought I was teaching here." John taps his clenched fist on the table.
>
> "You're learning to teach. Much of what you're doing is still inadequate, so you need to be knocked down a peg sometimes. You resist my suggestions. How will you learn to teach if you don't model or even listen? You're a little too certain of yourself." (262)

This is not as bad and as uncertain as it can get in a relationship between a student teacher and a cooperating teacher, but it is certainly bad. Neither John nor Mr. McMurtrey are able to make sense of this conflict in a rational way and, as Vinz understatedly points out, "neither John nor Mr. McMurtrey were willing to suggest that it might be important to talk about their different philosophies" (262). What we have instead is a struggle for power and control in the meeting of two rigid and deeply divided minds, neither one of which seems, at this point, even remotely capable of opening to the other. John is nowhere even remotely close to finding an occasion to begin here, yet if he wants to survive, he must. There is no tomorrow.

The dilemmas of Regina and John, of course, only hint at the wide range of uncertainty that accompanies student teaching. Overcontrolling cooperating teachers and clashes of ideological will are only two variables. Consider, as just one contrasting example, the uncertainty that Amanda faced in her student teaching:

> [For my student teaching] I was assigned five sophomore English classes, so I had one preparation. But a lot of students. I walked in the first day. My cooperating teacher was doing *Julius Caesar*. They were in the middle of Antony's funeral oration. She handed me the book and said, "We're right here," and waited for me to take over. Fortunately, I had read the play recently and knew exactly what to do with it, spent ten minutes drawing the kids in, stopping every ten lines or so and making sure we knew what we were talking about, and she left the room. And never came back. Never watched me teach. She was trying to get her master's and wanted to write her thesis. She had about eight weeks to do it and was teaching full time. So she went down to the teacher's lounge and wrote her thesis eight hours a day while I taught. At the end of the day she would come back to the room, take me to the nearest place, order two Cokes, and we would sit for an hour or two hours and talk about what had happened. It was like somebody threw me into water when I couldn't swim. I learned an enormous amount about teaching but I made every mistake you could make. One of my first, I remember, was a kid passing a note. I went back and tried to take the note and he wouldn't give it to me. I said, "Either give me that note or get out of here." Well, of course he got out of there. He went home. She said, "Well, here's what you learned from that. If you give two alternatives you have to be ready to take either of them." I never forgot that lesson.

Ha-ha. You don't give choices any more.

Ha-ha. Yeah. Unless I give two choices and I want both of them!

Out on the road when there are large numbers of "Bears" patrolling a stretch of road (as there always seem to be on I-80 in Illinois from the river to mile marker 125) and pulling vehicles over, drivers will comment wryly on their CB radios about how happy they are that the state troopers are providing so much "police protection." Regina and John, likewise, have plenty of police protection, with their supervisors and two highly involved cooperating teachers trying to do their thinking for them, as well as Ruth Vinz recording everything for posterity. My guess is that they would have been more than glad for a taste of the "sink-or-swim" experience that Amanda had in her student teaching. It is also the case that, at the time anyway, Amanda might not have minded having a bit of the helping-hand-strikes-again level of attention that Regina and John experienced. The point, however, is not how to imagine or design or attain some ideal level of comfort in student teaching, but to understand the ultimate futility of that and to begin living with the uncertainty that is central to the teacher's practice and life.

The closer my students get to student teaching the more they want to know what it will be like and the more detailed they want my explanations to be. "How many classes will I teach?" "How many preparations will I have?" "Will I be following my cooperating teacher's curriculum or will I have to (or be allowed to) design my own?" "What should I wear on Fridays?" Even though I sincerely wish I could answer such questions when they are asked, no one ever knows exactly what student teaching will be like until it actually starts—any more than practicing teachers can construct their own schedules, handpick their students, and predict exactly what will happen at the beginning of the school year.

Who knows what will happen? One student teacher I had once was contentedly sitting at a table before school on the third day of the term when her cooperating teacher walked up and whispered in her ear that he just could not continue. He left, and it was show time. One veteran teacher I know prepared all summer to teach one set of classes only to discover in the middle of August that a colleague had resigned and that she would be reassigned to a whole new teaching schedule. Even though these are dramatic examples, they are not different in substance from the unexpected and uncertain circumstances that Regina, John, and Amanda met when they began their student teaching—and that every teacher meets at various points along the way.

The absolute predictability of unpredictability, of uncertainty, like the biological evolution of pheasants, is a cruel joke on quail hunters and other human beings who so crave certainty and who devote so much of their lives to ensuring it. Ironically, though, the more human beings have learned and the more control we have gained over the world in which we live, the more aware we must become of the ultimate uncertainty of our lives and our deaths.

Given the scope of this challenge, student teaching is an excellent and relatively safe occasion to make a strong beginning toward learning to live the uncertainties of the teacher's life. Unfortunately, as is the case with my own students, there are few specifics I can offer you at this point that you cannot get easily from traditional textbooks and academic materials—except for one really good piece of advice I got one time from an unlikely source.

Getting Weird

If I would have been able to talk with Regina, John, and Amanda before they started student teaching, I would have told them about a night when I was in college and attended a speech by Hunter S. Thompson, a writer who defies easy description. From out of the shots of whiskey and torrent of words, some of which I could understand, I saved one line: "WHEN THE GOING GETS WEIRD, THE WEIRD TURN PRO." I know it is hard to take the whiskey-guzzling, gun-toting, and drug-addled Hunter Thompson seriously, but when it comes to situations that do not entirely make sense, he is a master. Even if it is by accident, he presents us with exactly the kind of mind that is useful for meeting the most confusing uncertainties of student teaching, finding a beginning, getting our clothes right, and passing through the final gate that is not really a gate. Here is how I interpret what Hunter Thompson said.

"When the Going Gets Weird"

The kinds of situations that Regina, John, and Amanda ended up in were weird, but not in the sense that they were unnatural or abnormal. If anything they were situations very similar to a myriad of others that commonly develop in classrooms every day. Their situations were weird in the sense that they were impossible to study and prepare for in advance. No matter how well John could work with texts and students, there was no way he could have been ready for Mr. McMurtrey. And no matter how well Amanda was prepared for Shakespeare, there was no way she could have been ready for her cooperating teacher to leave her alone. This is how it goes: in the normal everyday process of working with 150 or more young people and an assorted collection of teachers, administrators, supervisors, politicians, and parents, it is normal for the unexpected to occur and the going to get weird. Expect it. The weird is normal. What else could anyone reasonably anticipate with so many unpredictable humans brought together in one place? During our conversation, Amanda told me the story of a day when she was walking around her classroom helping her students with their work. At one point she looked down to step around a pile of books on the floor and saw the grip of a handgun protruding part way from a student's backpack. Suddenly the going got very weird. What to do?

"The Weird"

I cannot explain exactly who the weird are. All I can say for sure is that when you encounter or become the weird, you know it, and what makes the difference then is how you respond. Weirdness happens all the time. I remember, for example, one day during that difficult period when Michelle's oldest daughter was in the seventh grade and just getting to know me. I had done something or said something—exactly what it was

I can no longer remember—and her response was to curl her lip as only a seventh grader can curl a lip and say, "You're weird." For just a second her judgment made me feel bad: at the time there was nothing I wanted more than to be liked and accepted. But when I had a chance to think twice about what she had said, I had to agree with her. In the world as she saw it, there could only be two kinds of people: the weird and the normal. Normal was familiar, common, predictable. Normal food came from McDonald's or had canned soup, bread crumbs, and cheese in it. Weird was everything else that did not easily fit into her concept of normal. Weird had four pairs of waders, a set of black cushions, and a steel wok that cooked food that smelled like a nasty east wind. Normal was where she was and where she had come from. Weird lay in the direction she was headed, whether she knew it then or not. I was weird, I knew it, and there was nothing I could do about it but live it.

"Turn Pro"

The pro is the weird one who accepts it, who can handle the unexpected, who is at home with uncertainty and can live it. At the center of the turn is an open, loose, flexible mind reinforced with whatever courage and will you can muster, powered by attention and a sense of humor. Education students, student teachers, first-year teachers are always heading into the unfamiliar and are always the new, unfamiliar ones. Potentially, they are always the weird heading into the weird, and in order to begin they must find a way to make a home there. I am speaking of very practical matters. At the point I left off, John and Mr. McMurtrey were going nowhere. Their rigid, self-centered, one-dimensional minds were not even close to being capable of dealing with the weirdness they were going through. Like the fools they were, they were trying to make sense of weirdness and stake out a position on it, rather than trying to understand what was really going on, enter fully into it, and make the turn.

By contrast, I had a student teacher once who was assigned to an inner-city school. This student teacher had grown up in a rural area, had very little contact with minority students, and was especially frightened at the prospect of working with African Americans. Of course, it did not take her students more than a couple of days to recognize this student teacher's fear and, as students do everywhere, exploit it to the fullest by probing and testing her: they acted out, acted as if they could not understand her, spoke gibberish to her, pretended to be insulted when she could not understand their talk—they were merciless. The going was extremely weird. At first this student teacher did not respond very well and was easily intimidated. For a while I was very concerned that she would not survive, much less make a beginning, but I was at a loss about what to do. It was her riddle, and she had to solve it.

Then, luckily, things got even weirder. For no reason at all, other than to make a joke and torment her, one of the students in one of her classes called her a racist. I was there that day, and the effect of the student's pronouncement was electric. The student teacher, for all her discomfort and inexperience—as her students knew—was not racist. She was shocked and crushed by the accusation. She burst into tears and left the classroom.

At first I was afraid that she would just keep going, down the hall, past the welcome center, through the front door, and out of student teaching, the teaching life, and the weird altogether. But this did not happen. Not only did she come back, but she came back with a force I did not know she possessed. I could sense it when I saw her the next day, and when her difficult class came into the room, they could sense it too. They sat quietly—for them—and waited for her to begin, and when she began, what we all sensed became obvious: the student teacher had made the turn and was no longer afraid. Instead of her usual halting, insecure manner, she spoke strongly and with confidence. She spoke about herself, about her parents, her family, where she had come from. She told all of us for the first time what a challenge and what an opportunity it was for her to be student teaching where she was and what it was like for her to be teaching in a place so different from any she had ever known before. What she had to say and how she said it sat all of us right up in our seats and opened our eyes, and we all knew, all of us in our own individual ways, that we were in the presence of a new person who had never been in the classroom before and who had never been on Earth before either. This was a pro. This was a beginning.

There is no formula for this. Every teacher needs to figure out how to make the turn in the moment it needs to be made. Luckily, each one of us comes fully equipped with what we need. As a species, human beings have always been highly adaptable creatures with tough, open, flexible minds. When the lush, wet rain forests in Africa, our first homeland, receded, we learned how to begin anew on the open savannah and then begin again on the desert. When we spread out across other continents, we learned how to live with ice and snow and a range of hostile and extreme climates. When other species specialized, then overspecialized, and became finally extinct, we began to generalize, broaden the extent of our mental and physical capacities, grow, adapt, and, when we had to, change our environment. Humans are aggressive, opportunistic, intuitive, and capable of using their open, flexible minds to create new opportunities and beginnings. Even though these traits have often led us into evil and have caused great suffering, they are also great gifts that we can develop toward good ends and that we can use to accomplish much. When the going has gotten weird—really weird—we have always known how to turn pro. When we have been caught between fire and ice, we have always found the middle way between. And when we have been stopped, we have always found the way to begin.

Chapter Six

The Fourth Pillar: Stay on the Journey

How to differentiate staying on the journey from beginning the journey is more complex than it might appear on the surface. Frank's story, which I excerpted in Chapter 5, is an illustration of what I mean. For him, beginning and continuing are not two separate times in a teacher's career, but rather two closely interrelated processes that together define the dynamic action of a whole life:

> I've developed this pattern that every five years I like to try something different. I've had different careers within teaching, at least I consider them to be different careers. The first five years was that first job, which was more athletics. I coached year-round in those years. And for the next ten years I coached one sport and [designed and] taught a completely new class. And then I kind of became a utility player here. If they needed somebody to pick up an econ. class I picked it up, or U.S. history or government. So, I suppose, from my perspective I had a career the first place I taught, and then the next ten years here was a different career because it was a brand new curriculum. Everything was different. And then I had a career with at-risk. And now I'm back in the classroom, but I don't do anything I used to do. So I've changed again.

The ability to begin again is fundamental to Frank's being able to stay on the journey and live out his life as a teacher. Very few individuals can continue to do the same thing in the same way, no matter how rewarding it might be at first, day after day, year after year at the same level of excellence, intensity, and satisfaction. Even though Frank's teaching life really began when he entered the resource center, and even though he points to that as his greatest accomplishment, eventually he realized that he could not stay there forever:

> The thing that led me to get out of the resource center was its expense, its emotional expense. These were kids who, for whatever reason, were at risk. And you work with the kids and they work with you and you begin to see some progress, and then whatever it is that puts them at risk rears its head and they backslide. Sometimes further back than they were when you started. And while that's not their fault it's real expensive. It's hard to go in everyday and do that. And so I decided that to avoid burnout I would come back to the classroom.

The issue of emotional expense that Frank refers to here is not just idle chatter, and burnout is not just an abstract concept. Both have the feel of flesh and blood and both function as integral forces in the delicate balance between beginning and continuing that centers the movement, direction, and quality of a teacher's life. Following is an awkward moment in my conversation with Frank that shows what the full implications of staying on the journey are. Leading up to this excerpt, Frank and I had been talking about a friend of his who had left teaching after about fifteen years in order to make more money in a private corporation. Frank concluded his story by saying, "And he worked there for about five years and just totally hated it. It was dehumanizing. It was belittling and all those things. And he came back." Then, to my surprise, Frank followed that story about beginning again with a story that has a much different outcome and contains a powerful caution for anyone thinking about living the life of a teacher:

> And there's—I didn't know the man very well, a man I taught in the same building with who killed himself. And I didn't have any idea. I don't think anybody did at the time—
>
> *He committed suicide—*
>
> I don't know if it was because of—
>
> *While he was a teacher—*
>
> The stress of—you know—any of the stress of teaching—I know that he was a target of the kids—
>
> *Yeah.*
>
> You know, and there was a lot of derision from the kids aimed in his direction. I have no idea. I'm sure it had to play a part.
>
> *Yeah, it gets serious.*
>
> So yeah, it can drive you to the depths. You've seen it.
>
> *Yeah—well—yeah. I actually lost a student teacher once like that.*

Is that right? You know, you pick something that you think is going to be—it's a great profession and it's going to be good for you, and it isn't good for everybody.

Yeah, it's not good for everybody.

Just like every other profession isn't good for everybody. I don't think I'd make a very good man of the cloth.

I know I wouldn't. [Long silence.] What I find interesting is both the contrast and the similarity between you and these people you were talking about who left to do something else and then came back. They sound like you in a way, although you found a way to leave, come back, and begin again without ever really leaving.

Without ever leaving geographically, yeah.

Beginner's Mind

This continually renewing pattern of staying on the journey and living the teacher's life that emerges from my conversation with Frank is different from the simple, linear view that is so easy to get when we are in a teacher education program with its sequence of courses leading to (1) a degree, (2) certification, (3) a job, and (4) a career. Shunryu Suzuki, whose book, *Zen Mind, Beginner's Mind,* I discussed in Chapter 1, helps tease out the nature of this difference:

> In Japan we have the phrase *soshin* which means "beginner's mind." The goal of practice is always to keep our beginner's mind. Suppose you recite the [Heart] Sutra only once. It might be a very good recitation. But what would happen if you recited it twice, three times, four times, or more? You might easily lose your original attitude towards it. The same thing will happen in your other . . . Zen practices. For a while you will keep your beginner's mind, but if you continue to practice one, two, three years or more, although you may improve some, you are liable to lose the limitless meaning of original mind. . . . You should not lose your self-sufficient state of mind. This does not mean a closed mind, but actually an empty mind and a ready mind. If your mind is empty, it is always ready for anything; it is open to everything. In the beginner's mind there are many possibilities; in the expert's mind there are few. (1970, 21)

The point is that living the teacher's life is not, as a philosophy professor of mine used to say, "just one damn thing after another." We do not simply start off, get older and wiser, pass through the grades, get still older and wiser, and find more grades to pass. We do not just live our lives in a straight line—or at least we do not have to. Looked at from

Frank's perspective, as well as the perspective of beginner's mind, to stay on the journey is nothing other than to continually begin the journey. This, of course, is exactly what the Fundamental Principle teaches, too. Each *day* is a journey; each day we begin anew, and it is always possible to be at home in that beginning. This is also what Lao Tsu was getting at when he wrote "returning is the motion of the Tao." Always we return to live in the present moment and begin because that is the only place we can really live and continue on from.

You Can't Go Home Again

It might be tempting to consider this view of returning to begin as a literal return to where we started. But the common saying "You can't go home again" is true. Returning to the beginning is a return to a new beginning, to where you are now, not where you were. Your real home always moves with you. In her book, *The Zen Environment,* Marian Mountain, a student of Shunryu Suzuki, describes leaving her "old hometown." Part of what she means by this is a literal leave-taking, a journey to another place and another life. But a larger part of what she means is leaving the life and life of the mind that defined and controlled who she was before she was able to get out on her own. "Our old hometown," she writes, "is not just a place. It is also a state of mind, our egoistic description of reality, which limits our awareness by tethering it to words, concepts, and reasons" (1982, 8). A return to such a place, to where we were and who we were and what we thought, is the opposite of staying on the journey.

I think Frank does a good job of unpacking this distinction. The pattern of his teaching life demonstrates that any place in our teaching lives can become an old hometown that can grow into the place that hems us in, burns us out, kills us off. The resource center, as he explains it, gave him a new beginning in his teaching life by creating an occasion where it was possible for him to return to the fundamental basis of all teachers' practice: being and working with students. Yet, after several years, when working in the resource center became, as he put it, "too expensive," he needed to move on or risk getting stuck. What had started out as a new place for Frank had turned into an old hometown, and when that happened, he knew he had to leave and return to a new place where he would be able to begin as he had in the resource center six years before.

A verse translated by the other Suzuki, D. T. Suzuki, expresses one dimension of how this process works:

> Whatever and whenever the mind is found attached
> to anything

Make haste to detach yourself from it.
When you tarry for any length of time
It will turn again into your old hometown.
(Mountain 1982, 8)

Marian Mountain translates Suzuki's translation into terms more familiar to teachers this way:

> There are two excellent ways to go back to the beginning after having reached a goal. One is to become a teacher of beginning students. The other is to become a student in a new field. Both of these positions encourage us to return to our beginner's mind. . . . [T]his practice is important in all activities of our life—in politics, art, economics, science, business, marriage, child rearing, teaching, or in whatever other fields we might be engaged. (99)

It is easy to see how Frank's experience is directly related to this commentary. Not only has he found ways of staying alive professionally by returning again and again to new beginnings, but when he made his most enlightening return, to the resource center, it was to teach at-risk students who were, if any students ever were, beginning students. His move in that direction, as well as his experience starting new courses and programs, also represent disciplinary changes, new fields for him beyond his initial preparation in social studies and coaching. I do not know very much about the lives of Zen Masters, but when it comes to the lives of teachers, Frank seems to me to embody beginner's mind.

"There Are Times When"

For teachers determined to stay on the journey, the reality of tiring out, wearing out, or burning out can become a triggering mechanism that helps them begin to understand the need for returning to the beginning. Helen, who was completing her fifth year when I had a conversation with her, finds herself at just that point:

> I feel like the more I talk about teaching, even in the slightly fluffy courses I've been taking for my graduate program, the more excited I get about teaching. I like to learn new things, even if they're just small, that I can use in the classroom. . . .
>
> *What is it about where you are now that talking about your teaching or taking these courses makes you feel that way? And why is that important?*
>
> I guess I enjoy my job, but it's almost like a shot in the arm. A nice one that is. It's refreshing. Let's see, in the graduate course I took this fall the woman used a lot of cooperative learning. We got in groups. She had all these different methods for getting us in groups and assigning us parts and I brought that back to my classroom. It worked so well.

I'd been using cooperative learning for the last four years but had never used it so effectively. . . . At the end of last year I think I was experiencing a little bit of burnout. I had a particularly difficult class and it seemed like no matter what I did, it didn't work. Just with this one class. It kind of drained me. I went away thinking, "What was it about me? Why didn't this class go well? Why couldn't I really get a handle on the kids? Maybe I'm not such a good teacher."

Was this the first time you experienced a touch of burnout or uncertainty about how things were going for you or how you felt about your job?

Yes. Well, no, I shouldn't say that. I think there have been other times of uncertainty. . . . On and off I experience uncertainty, but I have a friend here who wants to get out of teaching so badly, and I can't say that I've ever experienced that.

Really? How long has she been teaching?

We started the same time. She's a year younger.

She's had it?

Yeah, regardless of whether she has a job or not she's going to sign up for a year's leave of absence next year and get out. She said, "There are times when I just want to slap kids."

How long do you see yourself teaching? Do you have any long-term plans?

Well, when I took courses in counseling and therapy, they spent so much time on burnout and avoiding burnout and all the things you could do. When I think about how that carries over to teaching and how it applies, I could see myself retiring as a teacher. But there are times when I think, "What if I don't want to? What can I do if I get to that point?" Right now I feel optimistic about it. But I've heard so many people say, "We need young teachers in there." Once I spoke at a young teachers' meeting. There was a woman there—I don't remember how old she was—I think she was fifty-five—she's been teaching for a long time. And she said, "Well, I think it's time for me to get out. As much as I've enjoyed it, we've got young teachers in my department, and I think they need that young blood, and I think I should just get out." And I thought to myself, "Well, do you think you should get out because other people think so, or do you think you should get out because you don't think you're doing a good job?" And then I asked myself, "Is it inevitable that as you get older you become a less effective teacher?" In twenty years I'm not going to be considered a young teacher, but hopefully I can change along with everything else and still continue to be a good teacher. I've always been fairly adaptable. I think I could do that. One never knows.

Helen's friend, it seems to me, is right. In the course of any journey "there are times when . . ." There are times when we all reach places in life and practice from which we do not know where to proceed. There are times when we become stuck, lost, or confused. There are times when we have just had it, cannot take it anymore, or do not know how we are going to go on. For some people, when those times come, the journey ends—even if they keep on teaching, going through the motions, collecting the paycheck, building up the retirement. Some decide to leave the teacher's life or—in extreme cases—even life itself behind. If when those times come, however, and a teacher decides for whatever reason to stay on the journey, the best way is to return to the beginning—wherever that happens to be at the time.

Following is part of a conversation I had with Isabelle, a teacher who understands this process well. When I talked with her, she was on the verge of retiring after a career spanning five decades, with the last thirty years in the same school.

How do you feel right now and what does it feel like to be about to retire?

Mixed. Mixed emotions. This has been a great part of my identity for a long time. And I will miss the classroom very much. But I'm going to do things that give me that same kind of association, that same kind of reward. I'm going to be working with youth in the church, I'm doing storytelling, and I'm going to the university free for classes. They allow retired people to audit classes and I'm going to take all kinds of things I couldn't fit in before. So, I'll have intellectual challenge still, I'll have adolescents to work with, and I'll be able to do some more writing.

From your perspective now, what's the most important thing you can think of to tell a student just entering this profession? A methods student, an undergraduate, a student teacher, or a first-year teacher?

That this isn't a profession you should get involved in unless you have stamina, really have passion for what you're teaching, and really like young people. I think those things are absolutely essential if you're going to find a compelling career in teaching.

Stamina, passion, liking young people.

I think that if any of those things is missing you won't really have a successful career.

Isabelle has all three of those traits in abundance, and finds in them the energy to discover a new beginning when she might reasonably be thinking about nothing other than the end of the journey. She is not retiring so much as she is starting two new teaching jobs—in the church and as a storyteller—and starting as well a whole new level of education. This is how it must always be for us if we want to stay on the journey. It is no different for a student teacher who has had a stressful, disastrous day than it is for the teacher retiring after a lifetime in the classroom. Always, "there are times when . . ." Always in the end there waits a beginning.

Using the Key

Obviously, it is much easier to talk about all this than it is to live it. Not everyone stays on the journey, nor should they: forced marches are death marches. In Chapter 4 I talked about several student teachers who failed, and I talked about an excellent teacher who burned out in what seemed to her an impossible job. Also, Frank and I talked about several teachers who were not able to find a new beginning the way Helen and Isabelle have. Why is it that some teachers are able to stay on the journey and others are not? Where is it that some teachers seek and find beginnings that others cannot find?

In the passage from *The Zen Environment* that I quoted earlier, Marian Mountain suggests that the practice of returning to the beginning is the "key" to surviving and staying on the journey in the whole range of human endeavor. This idea of a "key" is a very important one. The key is the device that opens the lock, locates and accesses the way, makes the way clear. If we have the key, we have the key to get out and the key to get in, the keys to the kingdom, or even the key that turns the "cosmic tumblers" that W. P. Kinsella writes about.

There is an old story about a famous monk that helps me better understand a further dimension of this idea of "key." Following is a version of this story as it was told by Dainin Katagiri in the introduction to *The Zen Environment*:

> One day, when he was practicing Zen in the monastery under his master Nansen, Joshu shut the kitchen door and stirred up the fire until volumes of smoke filled the room. Then Joshu shouted, "Fire! Fire! Put it out!" When all the monks and the Zen master hurried to the kitchen to help put out the fire, Joshu refused to open the door. Instead he said, nonchalantly, "If anyone can give me a word that will turn my delusion into enlightenment, I will open the door." Everyone was speechless. Except Nansen who silently handed Joshu a key through the kitchen window. With this key Joshu opened the door. (Katagiri 1982, xv)

Katagiri's commentary on this story points out its relevance for us in living the teacher's life:

> In this story Joshu and his master show us, by dramatic means, the whole problem of human suffering—what causes it and how to escape from it. Most people act just like Joshu. They close the door and

stir up the fire. They close their minds and stir up their desires. On the surface they may appear to be enjoying their lives, but inside they are suffering from the delusions that fill their minds. (xvi)

How often do all of us, regardless of how long we have lived and taught, find ourselves in a mess of no one's making but our own? It is not necessary for us to go out of our ways even a little bit to cause problems for ourselves the way Joshu does in this story. Sometimes, as Frank illustrates with his own story about the players who left their helmets at home, it can be the most fulfilling parts of our teaching lives we end up turning into the tightest traps. We are all perfectly capable of wandering into the hottest kitchen entirely on our own and then finding the way out blocked—or obscured—by our own actions. What we need then, as Nansen shows, is a key we can use to free ourselves. What I would like to do in the following sections is discuss examples of what, for teachers, some of these keys might be, how we might recognize them, and where we might go to look for them. Some of these keys are what we might expect, and open the way toward obviously positive actions. Some of them, however, like the first, "failure," seem to point in directions we do not want to go. The truth is, though, that while it is possible and desirable to follow the positive, it is often in the dead center of what we would have avoided if we could that we find the knowledge and the treasures that are the most valuable. Keats wrote it in his sonnet "To Homer":

> Aye, on the shores of darkness there is light
> And precipices of untrodden green;
> There is a budding morrow in midnight;
> There is a triple sight in blindness keen.
> ([1818] 1959, 157)

Failure

For me, failure was a key. I do not have much to add here to my discussion of failure in Chapter 1 other than to say that sometimes it is only when all is lost, when we seem to have been totally defeated, that we are able to find the way to go on. The cliche goes like this: never does a door close but that another one opens. Even though believing in such a possibility requires much more faith than good sense, if we do not believe it, we are lost, because being human means failing, and staying human means finding a way back from failure and staying on the journey. In a way, all teachers are Nansen, always ready—even if not always able—to provide the keys that their students need to free themselves. And all teachers, I guess, are also Joshu, in danger of locking themselves into a narrow, limited range of being, into the dark, murky kitchen of themselves, and then stirring up the fire. It is important to remember, though, it is in the darkness that the key shines the brightest.

Love

Love is a powerful key that opens many doors. In terms of teaching practice, love operates at many levels in many degrees. When Isabelle talks about "stamina, passion, and liking young people," one way of interpreting what she has to say is in terms of different ways of bringing love to teaching—or discovering love in teaching. To understand more of what Isabelle is getting at and how it helps define the key of love in a professional context, let me continue with the conversation I left off previously:

> I think that if any of those three [stamina, passion, liking young people] are missing you won't really have a successful career.
>
> *Talk to me about stamina.*
>
> Oh, I think that teaching is one of the hardest jobs in the world, and I think you have to be physically strong. I think you have to be healthy, I think you have to know a lot about stress management. You have to be willing to exercise and leave the problems of the kids behind. Because if you don't do that it can really wear you down. I don't think that kids have changed in the thirty years I've taught here, but the world they live in has changed. The problems they face have become more difficult. And they share them more readily, which can become a psychological burden. I think you have to have developed personal strength to handle those things. You have to be able to have a variety of techniques for stress management yourself so you don't become worn out.
>
> *What are some examples of what you're getting at?*
>
> I exercise. I either ride my bicycle or walk. I love walking to kind of change my day right after school. It becomes my day, no longer the students' day. I also think it's really important to have a source of entertainment and laughter in your life. And that gives you the strength to become a teacher. If you can't laugh you can't teach.
>
> *Ha-ha.*
>
> I think that's a great stress reducer—to look for humor in the most stressful parts of education. The faculty meetings, the site-based management council, the parents who are sometimes totally unaware, the political aspects. I think you have to make fun of those and laugh with your compatriots. Even be rowdy at faculty meetings. I think those things are great stress reducers and give you the strength back that's

depleted by teaching. I think one of the best things I've learned is to be nonconfrontational with kids. It gives you more strength if you can use humor and caring and common sense rather than confrontation. Also, I'm lucky to have a husband who will be a sounding board when I'm frustrated but who also makes me laugh and sing. You know, a hundred years from now who's going to know what that student was like? Let's go have a hot fudge sundae and forget it all.

Tell me about passion. What do you mean by passion?

I think you have to love what you teach. If you don't really think it's important and if you don't feel enthusiastic about it, kids will never buy it. Kids have a sense of whether you believe what you're saying or not. And I've seen teachers who don't care about what they're teaching anymore. How can they expect students to care?

When you talk about teachers who don't like what they're teaching anymore, why is that? Who are these people? What happens to them?

I think they're teachers who don't continue to grow and go back to school, lose their zest for what they're doing.

Or is it they don't go back to school because they've lost their zest?

I don't know which it is, but there are people who just put in the time, who complain about kids not listening instead of finding ways to engage them, who think kids are different now when they really aren't. You've always had to engage students. Attention span might be different now because of television, but there are a lot of teachers who, instead of coming into the teacher's lounge or to the faculty meetings really excited about what happened that day in the classroom come in with a "these kids" attitude. I think it's because they've lost their passion for what they're doing, either for the age that we're working with or for the material that they once found new, challenging, and exciting.

Liking young people. What is it you like about young people? Are there any specific qualities that young people have that you could point to?

Oh sure. Energy, honesty. I mean, they'll tell you whether they're bored or whether they like it. They give you constant reviews. Fourth hour will come in and say "Uhh, second hour said this wasn't very interesting today." "Well, guess what, I'm doing something different this hour."

Ha-ha. Yeah. I read the reviews and the show is bad.

So, I like that honesty and openness. I like the fact that they're honest in their approach to learning. They have a lot of energy. They're fun. Their ideas are so interesting. And they push you and challenge you and make you better. Kids keep pushing at you to make you grow, which I think is nice.

Isabelle's talk here is a veritable discourse on love in the teacher's life. Even when she is talking about "stamina," one of the things that she emphasizes is that in order to survive we must love ourselves and take care of ourselves. Giving to others is a central need in a teacher's life, but Isabelle also knows she needs to find time to give to herself, to give herself time and space and freedom to exercise the body and make physical and emotional deposits that offset the personal expenses teaching requires. Isabelle also touches on the importance of love in her relationship with her husband. Building a loving relationship with a partner is not easy, and it is not something everyone is able to do in a lifetime. Once someone sent me a fortune out of a Chinese fortune cookie that read, "True love is like ghosts; many have heard of them but few have seen them." This is true, I think, and there is no way you can plan for a love in your life. But if you are lucky enough you will find it, and it will be a great source of stamina and inspiration and make all dimensions of life more livable.

Isabelle also has an active sense of beginner's mind. Teachers, she says, do not just lack passion. They lose their passion for what they "once found new, challenging, and exciting." The key within the key of love that opens the way to maintaining contact with that passion, she goes on to say, is growth: "teachers who don't continue to grow and go back to school lose their zest for what they're doing." In order to stay alive, to grow, to stay on the journey it is necessary to return, to "go back," to go back to school, to go back and reconnect with the mind and energy of the beginning. The need for such reconnecting is nowhere more obvious than in the case of teachers who have come to dislike young people. I remember a teacher telling me once that she appreciated having snow days off because it increased the possibility that one of her students might get hit by a car and killed. Such talk is painful to listen to, and how teachers develop this way of thinking I am not sure. Part of it, I think, has to do with a breakdown in the necessary connection between the teacher's life in school and life out of school. Even though Isabelle is aware of the need to live a life apart from her students, she is able to practice love regardless of where she is or who she is with. She is settled. She lives a settled life with her husband, and she is able to carry that settledness into the classroom. Her life is not two lives, but one, and she is not two people, but one.

In the following conversation Gwen elaborates her view of where students fit in the life of the teacher. The question I asked her that led to this part of our conversation had to do with what she experienced as the rewards of teaching.

It's the kids, I guess. I feel like I still have a good rapport with kids. I feel like they still respond to me and what we're doing. I feel like they need somebody to do this. I was shopping last night and ran into a young man who graduated last year and he stopped and told me about a paper he was writing at college about our writing class and how it had changed his perspective. Just things like that. It's not monetary.

I know that.

Yeah. It's the fact that you feel you are making a difference.

How would you describe your basic approach to teaching, to working with students?

I remember our former principal describing me as "mothering" one time. And I think perhaps that I try a personal approach with the kids, that I can relate to them on a personal level and pull from what they have brought to class. That way I think they will be better able to relate to me and listen to what I have to offer.

Mothering? Umm . . .

I think you really have to want to do this, to see that there is a reason to be there, that you have a mission. And it has to be child-centered. It can't be that you're doing this for yourself. I wish that some administrators and central office people understood that too in the decisions that they make. Even though they pay lip service to doing it for the good of the students it's often done for the good of the balance sheet.

For Gwen, as for Isabelle, there is no hesitating in naming that which is most important—the students. Even though I have mentioned elsewhere in this book the tradition for "student-centeredness" in our discipline, Isabelle, Gwen, and other good teachers take the idea far beyond the level of a principle of pedagogy or educational theory. Gwen's metaphor of "mothering" speaks volumes about the nature and depth of her commitment and the continuity she has built across the different venues of her life. The journey she is staying on in her professional life is the same journey she is on in her personal life. This does not mean, of course, that she treats her students the same way she treats her children. What she is getting at here is an overall attitude of caring, affection, and acceptance taken up in a context where there are specific goals and specific needs for achieving them. At home or at school, the two worlds are not that far apart if our sense of practice is ample enough. Marian Mountain's term for a similar form of warm, genuine, but tough love is "grandmotherly kindness" (1982, 139).

Gwen's point about having developed a uniquely female approach to classroom management is worth noting. I think she is probably right. Men and women generally find different ways of approaching many of the tasks and practices of life, and both men and women have much to offer their students as well as learn from each other. But the most important point here lies beyond gender: everyone must find for himself or herself the kind of approach that works, the kind of approach that is an effective extension of his or her own person and personality. In the classroom, as in life, you must always be yourself. For Gwen it is mothering that works. For my own mother, it was not mothering—it was the direct approach. She tells of graduating from the State Teachers's College in Cedar Falls and taking her first teaching job, where she had a room full of "clodhoppers" who were older than she and twice her size. "And by God," she still says to this day, shaking her finger at me, "they learned to toe the line or I cut them down to size," which for her was about five feet and maybe one hundred pounds.

Amanda's way, perhaps uniquely for a woman, though not necessarily, lies through her life at home and the home she finds in her teaching life.

How would you describe the relationship between your professional life and your personal life? And how do you reconcile these two different lives?

Somebody was telling me recently that one of the characteristics of life in the nineties, I guess as a result of technology, is that work is becoming our home, and that home is becoming our work. The person who mentioned this was talking about marriages and how some people feel absolutely at home and natural . . . when they're at work. And then they go home and that's where the strain is. And I guess I've always had a crossover life between home and work. I don't know that they've ever been particularly separate because I have a passion for my job. My job has never—I can say *never*—felt like something I had to go do that I dreaded and that I only did to make money. I've had places I've liked working better than others. You know, years that have been better than others. But by and large it's been such a big part of my life. For instance, this week I took a big pile of stuff over that I usually hang on the walls at home to hang on the walls at school. And it felt very symbolic. I was very aware of the fact that I was transporting some of my home life over to that room and that I also have food and plants there and I have puzzles there.

It's really homey there.

I have music there. I want it to feel safe and I want it to feel comfortable. It caused a slight problem, not a big problem but a minor problem, in my marriage—that I was willing to give so much of myself to the job. There are only so many hours a day. There were times when I probably took time from the family to give to the students. It's very easy for it to consume me. When I was married, I needed to keep them more separate in my head than I do now. Now that I'm single I feel freed up to let my work take over as much as it needs to and I don't think it consumes me to the point where I'm a workaholic. I think I have life away from work. But it takes up much more of my time because I want it to than most people's jobs do. I love studying. I've always loved school, so it's hard to tell when I'm the teacher and when

I'm the student. I like learning, and teaching creates a feeling that I'm learning and so are the other people in the room. I'm learning from them and they're learning from me, and we're on separate searches. It's just a swirl. I'm not the authority and they're not the ignorant ones. I don't see it that way. It's just a search. But I love it. It's exciting to keep doing the search.

When you say "married to your job," what do you mean by that?

That I feel so joined. That it's such a part of my nature that I carry it with me wherever I go. I dream about it. I study my dreams and a good two-thirds of them are about school—I'm at school—or I've got some kids with me. Or I'm showing them how to do something—or I'm sorting out something. Last night I dreamed that I was cleaning off my desk at school and I had arranged books in an "L," the letter "L," for some reason. It's a part of who I am. When I'm shopping or on vacation or during the summer when you would think I might just be away from the job, my natural instinct is to either teach adults, teach more classes, or read the pile of books I've bought. Last night in somebody's garbage I picked up some fence to use with *Heart of Darkness*. It's part of the creativity of it, to think of some new thing to draw them in. I love that part of it. I'm still excited about that.

Even though Isabelle, Gwen, and Amanda are very different from one another, there is a single, graduated pattern that extends across the conversations I had with all three. What I am referring to as "love" Isabelle thinks of in her teaching practice as three specific and related traits: stamina, passion, and liking young people. Her sense of practice draws everyone within the web of importance, including Isabelle herself, who must be as well cared for as everyone else. Stamina, passion, and liking young people all flow from caring and compassion. Yet Isabelle is very careful to lay down a line of demarcation between self, home, and school. She needs time for herself, for her walking, for her husband and hot fudge sundaes.

Gwen, it seems, is willing to take the spirit of love one step further. After speaking in another part of our conversation about the importance of family in her life, she figuratively draws her students into a broader family circle by using the metaphor of mothering. Amanda is even more willing to blur the distinction between home and school, family and students. She is single; she is, if not married to her job, at least living with it in a committed relationship. Her students and her work, whether she is in school or out, occupy a good portion of her physical and mental life, both waking and sleeping. Clearly, in the terminology I am using here, she loves her work.

Love, in these three manifestations and in an infinite variety beyond, is an important key to staying on the journey. One summer I drove my pickup truck from Winter Park, Colorado, to Estes Park on Trail Ridge Road. Two experienced teachers rode with me in tight quarters. Trail Ridge is a beautiful mountain road, winding through heavy forest, running out above the timber line onto Alpine Tundra, and crossing the continental divide near Fall River Pass. Despite this rare beauty, and even though neither one of my passengers had ever been on this road before, most of the way up to the top their talk was of their classrooms, their plans for the upcoming year, their students. At the time this irritated me. I remember thinking that both of them were so blindly obsessed with their jobs that they should be pushed off the edge of the road just to put them out of their misery. Yet, as these things happen, when we were at the Fall River Pass Visitor's Center, at an elevation of around 13,000 feet, we ran into a student of one of these teachers along with the student's mother. The joy of that meeting, the friendship, the affection all around made me realize that I needed to think about these matters some more, that for a real teacher love of people and love of practice cannot be separated from such things as mountains, trees, or rivers, and that it must be enriching and life-sustaining to be able to live and be at home in such a wholehearted way.

To live with such love is to be blessed. Such love gives birth to compassion, understanding, respect, disciplined concern. It is not an accident that in my conversation with Amanda, without even thinking about it, she articulated exactly Paulo Freire's idea of liberatory teaching that I summarized in Chapter 4. All great teachers have the mind of great teachers. To live and work with such love is to return always to that mind, to love, to the beginning mind of love. Without this there is no way to stay on the journey.

Finding Balance in Hard Work

Teaching is hard work, no doubt about it, and one important key is the ability and willingness to work hard. Yet there is a difference between work and labor, and the real challenge is to find a balanced way to work that recognizes the presence of charity at home. Many outsiders have the idea that teaching is a relatively easy profession with a seven- or eight-hour workday, a five-day week, and a nine-month year. This is deluded and ignorant thinking. Cathy, who was just finishing her second year when I talked with her, spoke about the surprisingly difficult demands of student teaching. Then she went on to say that

> even student teaching, I don't think, can prepare you for when it's your own. When it's your own, the first year, is really what needs to be experienced. . . . For me, personally, it was hectic. I mean, I was [at

school] by 7:00 or 7:15 A.M. and I [stayed there] until 7:00 or 7:15 P.M. I have the luxury of doing that right now because it's just me. I don't have a family, I'm not dating anybody, I don't have any children, or any of that. So, it was OK. But even my Saturdays were consumed. My Sundays were consumed. . . . By October—I thought—OK, we've got to do something here. Forget it. So I always tried to keep Saturdays open and one night a weekend when I went out. I had dinner with my friends, I shot pool, or whatever. But Sunday was still my day with school. So it was Sunday through Friday—really—we don't leave at 3:05, you know. . . .

This year is different in some ways, but it's still a hectic schedule. Up at 6:15, to school by 7:15, and then piecing the day together. . . . I'm good in the mornings, I'm better in the mornings, and I'm more organized in the mornings. Then boom, I teach. And then I have a prep hour, which is normally spent grading. Or running around dealing with that "outside" stuff. And then class, class, class, class, class, and then on an average day I'm probably out of the building by 5:00. And that's when I'm pretty much together. So I'll clean up the room, set up things for people who are absent, piece together what I'm going to do tomorrow for probably one class. Then I go home and I do my personal stuff like run, have a meal—I do eat—and then watch the news or something. Normally by 7:00 I'm back at the school work. And then I stop school work by 9:00 or 9:30, maybe watch a half hour of something on TV. Isn't it funny—I've talked to other people who do it—but I feel guilty when I'm not working. And my mom even said, "Honey, you don't work all the time."

The schedule Cathy describes here seems to me like the schedules of most beginning—and many experienced—teachers: mostly work with extra work thrown in on the weekends. This imbalance is necessary for most teachers the first year. Toward the end of her second year, though, Cathy is beginning to realize that she needs to make adjustments:

As I said, I have the luxury right now of just me. So, diving into my professional life is great right now. But I also do it because my personal life—I don't know if I want to use the word *lonely*, because I don't see myself as a lonely person, because I'm not. But there are some things to say. I was dating someone when I moved here. It turned into a long-distance thing. I spent my weekends consumed with school. That was hard. That put a strain on us. And I think I'm at the point now where I have a grip on my confidence and a grip on my organization. And a grip on a lot of those other things. There's a part of me saying, "You know, it's time for you to get a personal life." And we're talking love life and just working on that side of it. Right now I feel like I have a pretty good balance in my life, but it's pretty easy for me to crawl into my profession, to crawl into school work if I get lonely or bored.

Well, it's always there; it doesn't go away.

I don't think my life is hurt by my profession, but I do need to find a little more balance.

This part of my conversation with Cathy is full of turns. I get the feeling that she is putting more effort into convincing herself that the way she is living her life right now is acceptable than she is into actually believing it. At the same time, though, I admire her ability to raise this issue to prominent awareness and to focus on the key of balance. I also admire the way that her awareness of balance in her personal life is growing along with her awareness of balance in her teaching practice:

> Sometimes I get disillusioned with other teachers, because I don't think they're really teaching. Now, there are days when I lecture. I don't know how much learning goes on when you lecture. But I think everybody should have the opportunity to break into groups or to do a presentation and to learn the way that they can learn best, whether it be through speaking or art or something like that. So I try to do these things. [My first year] was hard for me because you want to hold tight on the reins. You want to lecture, you want to pass out those worksheets. You want to do it that way.

In this part of our conversation, Cathy is focusing on two important themes in this book, survival and attention. As Frank observed in Chapter 5, beginning teachers are rightly concerned with survival and tend to think of themselves and what will work for them before focusing on what is happening with their students. Like Frank, Cathy turned first to highly teacher-centered activities that gave her maximum control over her classroom. But also like Frank, but more quickly, as she gained confidence and experience, Cathy began searching for ways to balance her classroom approach by turning back to her teacher education courses. When I asked her where she got the idea for shifting the center of her classroom from herself in the direction of her students, she said:

> Actually, methods classes. A lot of my teachers there said it's OK not to be in control. And they talked to us a lot about this whole concept of being a mediator as opposed to a knowledge base. And we've all been taught and we've all seen teachers who are the pillars of knowledge and who toss the information out. But I think as I've gone on I've also seen teachers say, "Here you go. Figure it out." Kids have a hard time with that. I've had kids say to me, "Hey, you're the teacher. Don't you know the answer to that?" Last year I found myself thinking, "Now, they can't explore this too much," or "they can explore this much and I'll fill in the blanks." This year . . . I'll say, "Here it is. Here are some things I want you to hit." And that is a very freeing experience. I don't have to do it all. I shouldn't have to do it all.

The need for balance is where you find it, in negotiating the distance between home and school or in formulating classroom practice. John and Regina, whom I discussed in Chapter 5, were just becoming acquainted with the dangers of imbalance. Cathy, after nearly two years' experience, is coming to see firsthand what Amanda and Frank in thirty years have come to know intimately: both teachers and students are learners in the classroom, and there is a need to find balance by weighing the teacher's responsibility in the classroom with the students'. A balanced practice is one in which everyone, students and teachers, are doing their parts and carrying their shares of the burden and responsibility for learning. Travelers on journeys organized along those lines have a chance of going the distance. Having a love life does not hurt either.

I want to turn next to my conversation with Emily, who gives us a broader perspective on Cathy's evolving understanding of balance:

> My first year was a fog to me. I was so busy and they made me do so much I didn't have time to be scared. I had four preps every semester. When I look back on that now, I don't really know how I survived. And I wrote the curriculum for every single one of those classes because I had no textbooks. I spent most of my weekends just preparing. I was at school at 6:30 every morning and I usually left about 9:00 at night. I couldn't have my practices for fine arts right after school. It had to be at 7:00 every night. So I generally stayed until 5:00, went home real quick, and then went back to school by 6:00. I really felt like I was successful. I had a lot of energy. I was the youngest teacher in the school and so kids wanted to work with me. I didn't have to go out and recruit people. They were just there. I became really comfortable there in just two years, and that was one of the reasons I knew I had to move. I had everything there I ever wanted, and there was nobody there pushing me to be more. It was too easy for me to just keep doing what I was doing and not make myself go further.

What's wrong with achieving a level of comfort like that?

> For me, that's not the way I've ever operated. Familiarity is good, but being comfortable, I think, could be stagnant. It could stagnate you.

So you don't like to be comfortable?

> Not in my job. My personal life, yes. But in my job I want to feel like there's somebody better than me pushing me all of the time. All of the time. That there's somebody who *could* push me to be better. I want to work with people—and this is one of the reasons I came here—who are always looking for new things and who aren't afraid of change. Maybe that's it. It's not being comfortable. I like to change once in a while. And where I was nobody wanted to change. I found my niche there, and everybody was totally satisfied with what I was doing and

everybody thought it was great. And I could have stayed there and done exactly the same thing for the next thirty years and nobody would have questioned it.

Emily and Cathy both had challenging first years. Both of them found that in order to survive they needed to sink their entire lives into their work. Both of them, though, before too long began to realize that, even if it is temporarily necessary, such a one-sided, unbalanced life is not worth living. Both went looking for balance. Cathy turned her attention to two forms of change. One was a straightforward effort to seek a more comfortable balance between home and school. The second was an effort to create a more balanced, student-centered classroom environment. In addition, soon after my conversation with her, Cathy took a job in another school district where she felt it would be easier to construct the sort of teaching life she wanted to have. Emily also changed jobs after two years. Even though she very well might have stayed in the same place for thirty years, Emily sought a different sort of equilibrium than she could gain by stasis. To balance scales means to move weights around. To balance means change.

Here is the teaching life Emily is living now and how she currently defines balance in her life:

This is the farm girl in me. I get up between 4:00 and 4:30 every morning. And I work out before I come to school, and I'm at school between 6:30 and 7:00.

What's your workout?

And hour of aerobics or a run if it's nice out. And that is a huge stress relief for me. My students know when I don't work out. In fact they ask me, "You didn't work out today, did you?" It's a big psychological thing for me, but it's more than that; it's physiological. I truly believe that I get something from exercising.

Yeah. I have to work out every day too.

I'd go crazy if I didn't. And it has to be in the morning that I do aerobics.

Mine doesn't.

Now, I bodybuild on Monday, Wednesday, and Friday. I consider it not weight lifting. It's more than that, because I do it for an hour and a half to two hours, from 5:30 to 7:30 or from 5:00 to 7:00 depending on my coaching schedule. And if I can't do it because we have a track meet, then I work my schedule around that. And I make sure I do it at least twice a week.

Do you go to the gym and work out?

I go to the Fitness Center. I have a partner there, and that's a social outlet for me too because it's all adults. A lot of my students say, "Why don't you lift at the Y?" The reason I don't lift at the Y is because when I leave school at night I want to be with my adult friends and not my students. One of the things I've learned is that you can be good at what you do and give a lot to the kids, but you can forget who you are also, and I did that for two years. Now, I make sure I get away from my students at night and I'm with adult company. Because I need that.

You say, "you forget who you are." What do you mean by that?

I forget that it's OK for me to go and do things away from school. If my students ask me to do something and I have plans for myself it's OK for me to say, "I can't do this." The first two years I think I felt like I had to say "yes" because I was still establishing myself. You cannot say "yes" to everybody all the time, because if you forget who you are then you can't be any good for anybody else. Period.

Tell me more about your daily schedule. You get up. You work out. Then what? Do you eat breakfast?

Every day.

What do you eat for breakfast?

Usually cereal. Just a bowl of cereal.

What kind of cereal?

Umm. Depends on what I feel like buying that week. I really like Frosted Flakes.

I was afraid of that. I wanted you to say "whole-grain granola" or something like that.

But I like Life, Grapenuts, and stuff like that. And if I don't have time, and there are days when I don't, then I make sure I eat something. I grab a banana and eat it in my office. I have fruit that I bring to school if I don't have time to eat at home. And I always make sure I eat lunch. I never skip lunch. Then at 3:00 I either go to track or work speech and debate until 5:00 or 5:30, and then I go to work out. Then I go home. And then I usually correct papers—I try to work at least an hour on something, but I never work past 9:30 on school work. Never.

Never?

It's my rule. My dad taught me that in high school. I'm a morning person. He said, "You'll get twice as much done if you'll get up in the morning. That's why I get here at 6:30 in the morning. I can get more done from 6:30 to 7:00—in thirty minutes—than other people can get done in an hour to an hour-and-a-half's work at night.

Emily's day is a busy one. Her energy level is high, and she is a highly motivated professional. What she says resonates in many different ways with Cathy's sense of life and practice and with Isabelle's as well. Even though they are at opposite ends of their teaching lives, Emily and Isabelle have much in common in the way they understand balance—between home and school, between rest and exercise, labor and recreation, adults and young people. Beginning the journey or drawing toward the end—it makes no difference: balance, balance, always seeking balance. In the practice and life of a teacher these kinds of issues are every bit as important as those issues that are commonly discussed in textbooks and methods courses. Living the life of a teacher is about balance as much as it is about anything else.

Which brings me back to Amanda. Amanda, it seems, has tipped the balance quite a bit in one direction and is moving toward erasing the line that Isabelle, Emily, Cathy, as well as most other teachers I have talked with, want to maintain between school life and personal life. In the following excerpt Amanda describes her day and the stresses of her teaching life, and although on the surface it seems similar to Cathy and Emily's days, clearly she has a much different understanding of how she is living and how she is living with her work.

> I get up at 5:00. I punch the coffee pot. As soon as the coffee's dripped I either read student papers—I respond to them on cassette tapes, so I talk into the tape. I'd say I spend an average of ten to twelve minutes on a paper. I either sit and do papers or read preparation for my AP senior class until about 6:30. I put in about an hour to an hour and a half before school each morning, and it's a very productive time, because I can do more mental work than I can at night when I'm tired. I have four preparations and a coordinator's position. I'm never still; I get to school and I'm on the go all the time. . . . So my work day is a lot of reading, a lot of discussion, bringing in things. I do physical things in class. I want experience in the classroom besides reading and writing experience. I want them touching things and hearing things— this week we brought in coffins for Romeo and Juliet. We brought cake for Shakespeare's birthday. Objects. So I do hauling, moving things. . . . I have such bright students, and I feel responsible for not boring them. . . . It's a lot of work. I take a couple of hours after school. I cook a real dinner, take a break. But I work at night. Two to three hours I would say—usually. So it's a hard day, and I generally work Sunday on school work. This is a harder year than usual, but there's always that backlog of reading. I also work with a group of teachers, facilitators, who teach adults, and that's actually two other workshops. One is an ongoing literary workshop that we do three times a year—reading the classics. I think we've done five of them. And that's always four to five books for that.

> *So, how do you perceive the stresses of your job?*

> It's fast-moving. There's something going on every second without letup, so it's important to fully take in—and this touches on my Zen

practice—and pay attention to what I'm doing every moment. If I'm talking to somebody I want to give them my full attention and to give full attention to each of the moments, which often means letting go of something that just happened. The letting go part is difficult. The practice has helped tremendously, the Zen practice, because I'm aware that—I can't even remember this year getting angry. I look at stress in a very different way. Most days I'm not aware of something I'd call stress except in the sense that there's a demand being placed on me. It's not unpleasant. It's like a guitar string that gets just tight enough that you can pluck it. It feels good.

Amanda is not, as miscellaneous ancient sages might say, "someone to be judged by common standards." For her, the degree of separation, not only between life and work, but between self and other, seems less than for most others I know. Balance, or rather imbalance, does not seem to be a problem for her. Balance seems to be something she lives, and that living makes it possible for her to take in stride challenges and frustrations that would leave many of us in a sorry, stressed-out state. Though she has a strong personality and most definitely has a sense of self, Amanda is also one of the most selfless people I know. Not too long ago she decided to buy new furniture for her living room. She selected a set of LARGE Victorian-style pieces that no amount of furniture-hauling experience could ever equip me to properly describe. It was big furniture, and when the furniture delivery people arrived with it, it did not fit in the narrow front door of Amanda's apartment. The furniture had to go back. Now, this would have been a major setback for most people, but in Amanda's case the problem was complicated by the fact that prior to having the new furniture delivered she had given away her old furniture to a family of refugees from another country. No problem. She just went right on with her life as she had been living it—only without living room furniture. No complaints. No woe is me. No hurry to buy new furniture. I am not in a position to comment on Amanda's belief that her spiritual practice contributes to her ability to live comfortably in her teaching life. I do not understand cause and effect in these matters. I do believe, though, that Amanda has been able to find a way to live out in her relationships with other people some measure of a basic Zen teaching I referred to earlier, which goes in part: "To study the Way is to study the self. To study the self is to forget the self." Amanda does devote a good share of her life to studying herself: she practices meditation, she studies her dreams, and she pays close attention to what is going on around her. When I talk with Amanda and visit her classroom, she seems engaged and at ease in what she does. Who she is and what she thinks about herself do not seem to get in the way of her ability to live fully in the world and to balance and integrate that living with her teaching practice. Regardless of how long she has stayed on the journey, Amanda still communicates a sense of joy and excitement that is more settled but not wholly unlike what I see and hear when I talk and work with beginning teachers.

Isolation, Fear

These, like failure, are the keys that we wish we could do without, but that we need to know how to use for those times the heat and the smoke in the kitchen grow too great to bear. Finding, recognizing, and then doing something about isolation, fear, and the other negative feelings that arise in our lives and practice can help us unlock the mysteries of ourselves and discover that each one of us—and no one else—is responsible for the way we live. No one in this world gets a ready-made life for free: everyone must make a life through the practices of living and working every day. When we find isolation and fear in our way, we can be sure we are on the right path because all ways to everywhere lead through them.

Isolation, if not fear, is actually built into the school day. In most schools teachers each have their own room, and for six or seven out of seven or eight class periods a day individual teachers are in their own rooms working apart from colleagues and the support of others. During the one, or maybe two, planning periods a day each teacher has, there is little time for collegial contacts and mutual support. Some schools—and in the area where I work these are primarily middle schools—are organized on the basis of faculty "teams" made up of teachers from across the curriculum who all work with the same group of 100 to 120 students. The schedule in these schools is much more open to collegial relationships and professional support than more traditional institutional arrangements. The schedules in teamed schools provide team members with at least two planning periods. One planning period is designated for team meetings in which teachers discuss curricular and procedural issues as well as individual students. The other planning period is left open to provide teachers with time to work individually or to develop self-sponsored projects with other team members.

Despite the fact that there are various administrative strategies like teaming that can ease a teacher's isolation, none of them go all the way toward solving the problem. In most places professional contact is still limited to those individuals whom the schedulers put together, and rarely are the teachers the schedulers. Recently, I have noticed a tendency on the part of a few cash-strapped districts to eliminate the extra planning period in teamed schools. When this happens, since team meetings still must occur, the schedule becomes tighter than under the traditional system. Many teachers, regardless of how their daily schedules are set up, must rely on the time before and after school and on weekends for working with colleagues or for serious, long-term projects. When the time constraints of extracurricular activities, meetings, and coaching are added into this mix, it is easy to understand how frustrating the situation can become for teachers to find time for professional and personal business.

Problems like these are capable of stopping teachers early in their careers. Fortunately, they are also capable of unlocking inner resources that many people do not know they have until they need to find them or else. Cathy, for example, in the conversation I included earlier, does not want to admit that she is isolated in her work and that her life is "lonely." Yet, everything she says about her first two years and her plans for a third suggest that she has come to the realization that her life is, in fact, lonely and unbalanced. It might be easy for her and other young teachers in her position to feel bad about this situation, to feel self-pity, to quit the journey that does not seem worth making. Instead, Cathy decides that the problem is not so much with the job or the journey but with the journeyer herself, and that in order to go on she must find a way to rebuild and balance her life. This kind of understanding is a healthy expression, I think, of "beginner's mind," and in Cathy I see a teacher who is using her sense of isolation and dissatisfaction as a way to return to the roots of her most personal needs and her desire to begin the journey in the first place. In a way, she is beginning to sound a bit like Isabelle when Isabelle speaks of being highly aware of what she needs to do to meet the challenges inherent in retirement. Retirement, like the school, is an institution that is dangerously capable of isolating individuals and leaving them alone to face a world that is changing at an uncomfortably rapid rate.

Helen, after five years of teaching, understands isolation too. When I asked her how many opportunities she has to work with her colleagues she replied,

> Before this year we had very few. We implemented a program this year in which the students are released every Wednesday at 2:00. So, once a month we have to get together as a district and then we have to get together in departments a second time, as a school a third time, and then the fourth time we get to meet—we *have* to collaborate with someone, make a meeting with a colleague, plan a meeting, get together, and those have been rewarding. I've been able to work with a guy who's been teaching media for a long time. I know very little about media. That's been kind of fun. But other than that, especially before this year, we've had so little time, maybe a few minutes in the morning before the contract day starts. That may not be a big deal, but we were not given the time.

Do you feel any sense of isolation . . . in the . . . small amount of time you have to spend with others?

Yes. Definitely. I guess I tune it out because we've never had much time. I don't think about it very often, but just last week during final exams we happened to have a time [when we went] over to the library. And this librarian was going to treat these kids who had gone and done reading at the elementary school. But no kids showed up and she had something like twenty-five pizzas. So, practically the entire faculty was in the library. It was like a fellowship deal. We just kind of stood around and looked at each other. We'd never had such a thing where we could just be together like that. It was just really odd. Yeah, definitely you feel isolated, and especially . . . from the administration. . . . Last year, I hadn't seen the principal in my room since my first year. He hadn't stepped foot in and made any comments to me. And he came in last year because I had two broken desks. I had these cruddy wooden desks. And he said, "What's going on here with these desks?" I said, "What do you mean? These desks are old." I don't know how old they were, but they're terrible. He said, "I'm just wondering why there are these two broken desks in your room." I just took that kind of personally. "You haven't been in to evaluate my teaching, you haven't said word one about good, bad. And now you're in here talking about desks being broken."

At least for the time being things are changing in Helen's school. With the new early release system, the teachers have a small amount of time each month they can spend on self-sponsored collegial activities. Yet one can't help getting the sense that this change is at best a meager one that has come much later than it might have. Despite saying that she welcomes the new opportunities to meet with colleagues, Helen uses and emphasizes language like, "we *have* to get together" and "we *have* to collaborate," making it sound as if collegiality is just another administratively imposed task that the teachers, as professionals, are not consulted on and lack ownership and control over. Similarly, her disgust at what I would call, at best, the lax professionalism of her desk-jockey principal suggests an unhealthy sort of isolation between faculty and administration. Unfortunately, this kind of separation between the two groups is all too common in many schools, where every few years the teachers must sit down across the bargaining table from the administrators and negotiate a union contract that spells out every point from class size, to sick days, to professional leave, to what to wear on Friday.

The scene that Helen depicts in the library when the collected faculty of the high school suddenly comes face to face with each other over a steaming pile of pizza is poignant and sad. These are professionals with years of education and many more years of valuable experience.

Thousands of students have depended on these teachers for significant parts of their lives. Some of these teachers have literally *saved* students' lives. The collective contribution of this group of professionals cannot be rivalled by any other group in their community, yet the system under which they work keeps them so isolated from each other that when they meet by chance in a relaxed school setting without management running the show, they do not know quite what to do with each other. What other group of professionals is subjected to the same shabby treatment? And what is the solution to the problem?

Helen's immediate solution, as she said, is to go to graduate school and to pursue professional contacts and advancement outside the school. Another broader, longer-term solution is for faculty to press for scheduling that permits them to work together as colleagues and for contracts that contain adequate release time and financial support to attend professional conferences and meetings. None of these solutions nor any other solutions, though, are likely to come without a great deal of effort over an extended period of time. There is a long tradition for keeping teachers "in their place" by isolating them in various ways. In the nineteenth century, female teachers were not allowed to marry and were required to live in the homes of school patrons. For a good part of the twentieth century teachers were not allowed to drink in public. I can remember what a stir it caused when my fifth-grade teacher used to go with her male friend to my father's bar. Isabelle told me that once, in the 1950s, she had signed a contract to teach in a school district only to have it withdrawn when she showed up in the fall pregnant with her first child. Even though it often does not seem like it, teachers have come a long way in establishing their professional autonomy. Yet, there is still a very long way to go before teachers like Helen and her colleagues gain sufficient control over their time and their professional lives so that meeting on their own without administrative supervision becomes a usual occurrence—just as it is for university faculty, physicians, lawyers, and other professionals. To get where they need to go, teachers must keep the pressure on, must keep showing up each day, and must stay on the journey.

Yet another way of saying this same thing is to say that teaching, like any day-in, day-out, year-in, year-out practice is a grind and that those who are the best teachers over the longest period of time are those who are tough enough to grind the institution down before they get ground down themselves. As Isabelle says, teaching takes stamina. It is not just a matter of how good you are, how smart you are, how innovative you are, how dedicated you are. To stay on the journey, what matters as much as anything else is how tough and strong you are. Often, what staying on the journey comes down to is a confrontation between the teacher's sense of isolation weighed against her or his love for the students, fears against hopes, exhaustion against commitment. This confrontation could come at any time or arise out of any set of circumstances, but whatever form it takes, it lies at the gateway that every teacher must pass through to continue on the way, the gateless gate of the self that always lies directly before us. Here, picking up on earlier passages, is Diane's story of how she passed through this gate:

> I think I stayed with it, even through pretty rough times, because I think it's a noble thing to do. I think that I can't do something where I don't feel like I'm making a real contribution. I need that. I need to feel that when I go to work each day I'm not just doing some menial job—that I'm affecting society somehow. And so I come back to that, that I make a difference somehow.

> *That's a much nobler purpose than I had when I started out.*

> Well, I'm not sure I had that right when I started out. I think that may have come later. I think when I started out I just sort of ended up in it, and it seemed to be something that I could do pretty well, so I kept doing it. And I didn't love it at first.

> *Really?*

> No. I did not. In fact, I was sick at my stomach every day on my way to school. I mean I felt really nervous and uptight.

> Really? *Where was your first job?*

> Well, I took over for the person that I did my student teaching with because she had a nervous breakdown.

> *Why did she have a nervous breakdown?*

> I don't know. I don't know. But I took over for her for one semester and then I got married and moved and taught [in the suburbs of a big city] for a long time until we moved here. And then I've taught here ever since.

> *What was so awful about your first job that it made you sick when you went to work?*

> Umm. It didn't happen in the job where I took over for my cooperating teacher. That was a small-town school. I knew the kids already. The [job that made me sick] was in the suburbs. I think the big thing is just being terrified of losing control. You know, not having control over the classroom, what was going on there. It never really happened, but I was afraid of it all the time, I think. That happened then, and then I stopped and had kids, finished my master's, and when I went back again I remember feeling really nervous. . . .

> *Why did you decide to go back after that first experience that was so difficult?*

Well, that's interesting. I think it was because I was good at it. And so even though it was stressful I just do this with myself, I suppose. Maybe I'm a glutton for punishment, but if it's a challenge I do it. And if I'm nervous about it then I conquer it. . . . That had a lot to do with my deciding to go back. I never considered not going back.

For me, Diane exemplifies what I mean by toughness: personal toughness, professional toughness, commitment—commitment to herself, her students, her practice. How many people, like Diane, would have been able to get up every day, deal with such blunt physical fear, and not only stay on the journey but make of it in the process a mission because she came to believe teaching is a noble thing to do? And she did it not just once; after a long period of respite, she came back for more.

At this point in our conversation I asked Diane about her work and teaching day. She went on to describe a 5:00 A.M. to bedtime schedule similar to Cathy, Emily, and Amanda's. Next, our talk shifted to the issue of finding a balance between teaching life and the rest of life. I asked her a question: "In a general way, how do you define your life outside teaching?" She responded by re-asking my question in a way that made more sense to her, and then moved on to a long, complicated answer that shows more clearly than any explanation I have ever heard how the need and the courage to respond to fear and stress can sustain us and lead us to deeper knowledge of ourselves and the lives we are living.

Do I have a life?

Yeah, besides teaching.

It's really hard. It's really hard to say I have a life outside of teaching. I'm really working on that. I'm really working to have a life outside of teaching. It generally consumes me. That's not good and I know that's not good. And I am *consciously* trying to change that. By taking time out to walk in the evenings. Or watching an occasional TV show. Or to do things on the weekends without bringing forty dozen papers with me. . . . So, you're talking to someone who has a really difficult time making a life. You know, I guess I'm at the point in my life where I'm thinking, "What do I have?" I haven't figured out what else to do. I'm just doing this. In the summer I love to garden. I like to be near water. I like to travel. . . . It's difficult. I have a hard time. Because even on weekends I spend an awful lot of time grading papers or preparing. And of course I always get myself into other things too—like another teacher and I are doing sessions [at state and national conferences], and we're arranging to have some writing consultants come in—it's my own fault; I don't give myself a break. So I must like doing this. Or I'm crazy.

Yeah. Probably one or the other. . . .

You also mentioned earlier that the first thing you do each morning is meditate. How does meditation function in your teaching practice? What kind of meditation are you doing?

Well, I read a book last summer. I can't think of the title right now. . . . It was on the best-seller list. The guy is an M.D. at Johns Hopkins. Something about mindfulness—anyway, I don't know what kind of meditation it is. I just know that at the back of the book there was a place where you could send for tapes. So I sent for tapes, because I had tried before just doing it on my own. . . . Well, anyway, I got these six tapes and I started with the twenty-minute ones. Or maybe ten, twenty, and thirty. So I started with the short ones and then moved to the thirty-minute ones. I don't know what kind of meditation it is, but it's not hokey. You know?

You don't chant sutras and burn incense?

No. It's just enough—there are just enough words on there to keep your mind focused on where you're supposed to be. And that's all. . . . There's nothing funny about this at all. So, it's amazing. I didn't think I'd get up for anything. And I really like this. Even this morning. I was really exhausted because I couldn't sleep last night. I probably had four hours. This morning I got up a little early and I thought, "Oh, I'm so tired." But it's nice in that—it's sort of this realm between sleep and wakefulness. So it sort of eases me into the day.

So how do you see this functioning in your job?

Well, that's one way. It eases me into wakefulness. The other thing is that even throughout the day it reminds me that this all changes. That we're living now. And that even in the midst of—here's a story. I was in this eighth-grade class and, you know, I normally don't teach junior high. I kind of forgot how they are. And I was trying to help a student—I was leaning over, obviously talking to this girl. Around me there were probably four other ones tugging at my clothes saying Mrs. X, Mrs. X, Mrs. X. They're so self-centered at that age. And they didn't mean to be nasty or anything. They weren't even thinking about the fact that I was talking to somebody else. And so, it allowed me to just kind of step back from that situation and say, "This is funny, really." And then in a few minutes I could stand back with them and say, "Wait a minute, let's talk about what happened here." I think I'm living my life better and realizing, "Hey, this is it. This moment right now is it. And I have these papers but there'll be another moment. . Right now this is the moment." Somehow I think that this has helped me to do that. . . .

This may be a part of my struggle, too. To give myself some time. I wasn't having any time for me. And that's wrong. And [even though] it's time I'm taking out of my sleeping, that's the only time I can find, so that's when it is. But still, it's completely self-centered.

Yes, it's inherently self-centered, but somehow too I hear you saying that it's moving the edges of the center outward.

Yeah, and that's OK. I'm amazed, really. One of the things he says in the tape is that you shouldn't struggle to feel any particular way. So there's a part of it—and I'm thinking, "What is this?" You know? "There's nothing here." But I still feel like it has changed me. It's just really settled me over the last couple months.

I think I know what you mean. There's really no way to talk about it. I think that if you could talk about it, it wouldn't be what it is. It's something that happens beyond a conceptual or verbal level. And you can't really talk about it.

Yeah. I think that I've changed somehow. That often in the day I am being mindful of what is happening instead of fretting about what I haven't done or should do, which is generally what my life has been.

Yeah.

The old Puritan guilt trip.

At this point in our conversation it is easy to see that much has changed for Diane since the days she became sick to her stomach on her way to school in the morning. Yet, in contrast to Amanda, who seems to have not only balanced but integrated personal and professional life, Diane seems to sense that there is still something out of whack. She wonders about "having a life" at all. She asks "What do I have? I haven't figured out what else to do. . . . It's difficult. I have a hard time." These are questions that come straight from the heart of a serious traveler in the midst of a serious journey. She is trying, almost desperately, to locate herself, to figure out how she is doing, and to find the way that is the way on for her. Her brief experience with meditation suggests some interesting possibilities. There is something in it that she finds so compelling that she is willing to make a change in her lifestyle. It is also a practice that she feels she can take with her into her teaching that pulls the separate parts of her life together and gives her an understanding that she did not have before. When she talks about "living [her] life better" by realizing that "hey, this is it, this moment right now is it," what I hear are statements emerging from the growing awareness of someone who has moved much more than twenty years from the sort of life in which one gets sick at the mere thought that something might go wrong. And when she says that this "reminds me that all this changes, that we're living now," I see her coming into contact with the fundamental fact of our impermanence, the impermanence of our world, and the ever receding yet ever immediate destination of our journey. These, from my point of view, are profound insights, and the distance she had to travel to reach them more than worth the effort.

One dimension of all this that Diane is not coming in contact with is the question of "how much is enough?" When we had our conversation, she had been teaching for more than twenty years and, regardless of how many ways she had grown, she still had not been able to satisfy herself that she had a "life." Human beings can only do so much, and prayer or meditation go only so far in solving the problems we have in our lives and our world. Even though I did not mention it when I talked with her, Diane's struggles make me angry. Here we have a fine teacher and fine person, not unlike countless other fine teachers, struggling against circumstances, working conditions, and workloads that are nearly out of control. When is it time to change not only the shape of her personal life, but to seek the action of justice to relieve what is surely an oppressive regime that is serving neither teachers nor students? And, if that is not possible, when is it time for Diane radically to redirect her journey in a direction that, for her, will not only make living possible, but a life as well. As Helen said in our conversation, "there comes a time." What kind of time is coming for Diane?

Who knows? For the time being, however, Diane seems much more interested in finding the kind of balance that comes from centering teaching and attention on students and letting the larger questions ripen:

> You know how I was saying that at the beginning I was afraid of losing control? Well, I think something has changed . . . about my philosophy of teaching. It's not just for me. It used to be the teacher at the front of the classroom and the kids all out there, and "my job is to keep order in this place." And that's not so true now. It's a more student-centered class now. And so more things happen. It's more alive, and I expect that to happen. So, it sort of takes some pressure off of me. We're all working on this thing together. I think of the classroom as a sort of living, breathing organism and it works and functions together. Things go away, but it's exciting to see what can happen. And I think that has taken pressure off. It does cause other problems, but it's more exciting. And each hour is different and that didn't used to be. That's something that's really changed since I began.

> *Do you think a lot of that has to do with accumulated experience?*

> A lot of it, probably. I'm less uptight and more willing to take chances. But I know I can get them back again, too. So, that's the difference. They can be noisy for a while, and I know that when I say, "It's down to this," it's going to happen. And I don't think I knew that in the beginning.

> *Maybe that wasn't true at the beginning, either.*

> It probably wasn't, but I didn't dare find out.

So, how would you sum up the difference between a beginning teacher and an experienced teacher, or you as a beginning teacher and as an experienced teacher? Or is that a way you would approach talking about these changes?

No, I think that it has *some* to do with a beginning teacher and an experienced teacher. It has some to do with the fact that our whole—everyone's—philosophy of teaching has changed. [Long Pause] The beginning teacher has a harder time. He or she hasn't built any credibility. And that's hard. After you've been in a school for a while kids know your reputation. You have a chance to build a rapport with students. You've built up a reputation for yourself. It makes everything easier. When the kids come in they already know who I am and what to expect. I'd be a lousy sub. I would be because I'm not the kind of person who puts fear into anyone. The reason kids behave in my class is because we have this relationship with each other. And that doesn't happen in a day. That isn't easy for a young teacher because it takes a while. On the other hand, the young teacher has something I don't have, and that is *youth!*

But old and wily always beats young and fast.

There's something the young ones understand. They understand kids —maybe—better. Maybe they have an advantage.

Could be a disadvantage.

It could be. It could be.

There are two points in this part of our conversation that I think help sum up what I want to say about the keys of isolation and fear. The first point is that Diane's struggles have somehow led her to understand the central progressive reform agenda aimed at making a shift from a teacher-centered to a student-centered classroom. She understands it not so much as a *reform agenda,* though, as she does a natural outcome of mindful and persistent experience—of having traveled far enough and long enough under difficult circumstances to know what is going on and what is important. And what is important is not the teacher:

> You have to look at the kids. I had a student teacher last year who never looked at them. He never knew whether they were getting things or not. He couldn't see the glazed look in their eyes. Or the sparkle in their eyes. You have to get to know them, to respond to them all the time. We're not putting on a show up here. We're teaching. And that's different. And some get so wrapped up in *themselves* being in front of the classroom that they're not paying any attention to all those people who are out there.

Diane's position here, while it strongly reinforces the points about mindfulness and paying attention that I discussed in Chapter 4, as well as the insights Frank and Cathy achieved in their teaching practice, is not good news for Joy Ritchie, Dave Wilson, and the rest of us who want beginning teachers to go out into the world and work for progressive reforms. What Diane is suggesting is that progressive approaches to teaching practice do not easily emerge from the agendas of the teacher education program and the theory, pedagogy, and political imperatives that drive those agendas. At first there is too much that gets in the way of beginning teachers, from fear and the need to survive, to over-work and wandering attention, to allegiance to traditional, nonprogres-sive methodology. However, and this may be the good news, true and thoroughgoing progressive reform can certainly arise when it develops naturally out of a teacher's ability to understand self and students and to practice the life of teaching mindfully, returning always to the be-ginning point of attention, to the students themselves.

The second point I want to emphasize is painfully obvious and simple: "The beginning teacher has a harder time." This does not seem fair, but it is true. One of the reasons beginning teachers struggle with feelings like isolation and fear is because they are inexperienced people working in new and strange surroundings under difficult conditions. This is hard. Flat-out hard. Damn hard. But such a struggle and such a beginning are the keys to reaching everything that lies beyond. I remember years ago a University of Oklahoma quarterback wearing a neck band that had these words on it: "Hanka Yo." In an interview I heard him say that these words were from a Native American battle cry that meant "Clear the Way." Well, "Hanka Yo" then. Clear the way. The struggle itself is a necessary key to opening the way beyond it.

Change

Change is an important key to staying on the journey because it makes beginners of us. The following conversation picks up on the conversa-tion I had with Frank that opened this chapter. Here Frank is explain-ing what it would have been like if he had stayed in his first teaching assignment and had never had the opportunity to work in the resource center:

> If I was still teaching the first class I taught here I would definitely—I don't know what I would definitely—I just think that moving out of the paradigm, moving out of the box and being challenged has really improved my life. It's increased my stress. But I'm not sure it's bad stress.
>
> *What do you mean by that?*

Well, I think stress comes in two forms. It can be good or bad, I believe. For example, if you get a new job and you're going to come in here and your job is to teach American history, and you're so excited about it you just can't wait to get going and you're writing your curriculum and you're checking with everybody and you're going to libraries—that is stress. But I'm not sure it's negative stress.

What's the negative kind?

From my perspective, what characterizes negative stress is things that require me to use energy in negative ways. Worrying. Fear. Trying to keep up. When I don't really want to. Trying to put one foot in front of the other. . . . That's what would have happened to me if I would have stayed in that first course.

What would that have been like?

That would have been like, "How can I do this same thing—I can't teach this same thing. I don't want to teach the same thing that I taught last year." [Early in my career] I didn't ever push myself to change.

Hmm-mm.

I'd never been forced out of the box.

OK.

Nobody'd ever spit in my soup. And they spit in my soup when they said, "Frank, if you're going to work here next year you're going to be in the resource center.

Ha.

So I had to get a new bowl. And it is *the best thing* that ever happened to me. Although the first two years were hell.

Why so?

We were scared. We didn't know what we were doing. We were new at it. There wasn't any pattern to follow. I was a bit afraid of the kids, because a lot of these kids were hard-core kids. All those things added up.

Was that bad stress, then?

Ahh. Yeah. I think it was. By my definition it would have been.

When you're faced with that, how do you deal with it? How do you get out of that and into a more positive way of being?

For me it was just little bits at a time. Every little piece that was a success started to make me feel more confident. And the more confident I felt the more I felt, the more I felt, like, "OK, I'm safe here now. Now I can move out and start to do things that I think are going to help me and the kids." And so for me it was to get a firm footing.

There are three particularly important aspects of change that Frank provides for us here. The first is the point I began this section with: change creates a new beginning. For those of us just starting out, the changes may come rapidly and intensely, with campus course work leading to student teaching leading to the first full-time year. For experienced teachers change creates an occasion to begin, to reestablish contact with beginner's mind and so stay on the journey with a fresh step and new will to travel. Second, change pushes us. It challenges us—gets us out of the box as Frank says, puts us in situations where people are likely to spit in our soup. This is not fun—for a beginning teacher or for an experienced teacher. As Frank says, and as most other teachers would agree, "that first year was hell." Third, and this is closely related to the second point, movement through change and the stress of a new beginning can just as easily be slow movement as fast, seeming to occur in infinitesimal increments of time. How did Frank finally learn to live the life of the resource center teacher? The same way Diane learned to overcome her fear and establish herself. "Little bits at a time. Every little piece that was a success started to make me feel more confident," Frank says, and the more confident he became, the better footing he was able to gain and the safer he felt. These words, like Diane's, are the words of a courageous traveler who has crossed tough distances and has found his way and made it his own. What he is talking about here is moving very slowly, paying very close attention, and finding a home along the way—making a home along the way. The journey itself must be home. There is no other.

Amanda, like Frank, after more than thirty years of experience also recognizes that change is an important key:

> I think change is a real essential in this job to keep from becoming burned out. I think if you keep doing something new that you stay alive. There's a very short time when you can repeat something and get sharper and better at it without getting stale. And I think that is four to five years. Over that, if I'm doing the same thing year after year, day in and day out, I lose that edge because there's not much being asked of me. I can do it too easily, and I need to keep adding a little more challenge to it.

Helen, who has been teaching for five years and who might be becoming familiar with how long one can repeat the same thing, has some thoughts on this too. The following dialogue shows how she responded when I asked her to identify the one thing that she thinks it would be most important to communicate to a teacher just entering the profession. Even though she seems to feel her point is not particularly important, I think it is:

I would have to say—and this isn't anything profound—be flexible. And that's with students, with colleagues, with administrators. Really, that's what I'd say.

How do you cultivate flexibility?

Ha-ha. I don't know if you can.

Some people are born flexible, some people achieve flexibility, and some people have flexibility thrust upon them? How do you cultivate flexibility?

I don't know if you can cultivate it. In teaching, there are so many chances to get your feathers ruffled. We have constant interruptions. . . . Like yesterday. I'll bet we had ten to fifteen interruptions. Now, some teachers get very angry and upset about this. But unless you can do something about it—maybe if as a faculty we all hated it we could come down and protest and say, "please let's make a guideline or something." Then what? When students try to egg you on or try to bug you, you just have to come up with ways of dealing with it. Flexible. You can't just adhere to one rule with all students. This flexibility thing could just go on and on.

So, you have to come up with some way of dealing with it when you're confronted with a frustrating or difficult situation?

You can't blow up. You cannot blow up.

How would you describe the kind of skill that's involved in doing that? Suppose something happens and you're being guided by the principle of flexibility. What are the mechanisms of mind and body that you bring into operation at that kind of moment? Or do you have an awareness of that? ·

I guess the first thing I think is, "How can I best handle this, how can I handle this in a way that I feel good about?" Because sometimes you just want to scream something at the kid. I've done things and then I've wished, "Gee, I wish I hadn't done that. . . ." I don't feel right with what I've done, "I didn't mean that." And then I think that, "Gosh, if only I had thought longer." "Why am I acting this way?" So I guess all these things, "How, why, why am I acting this way?" It's just constant evaluation. All kinds of questions are going through my head. "How should I react? How do I want to react?" Checking in to ask, "If I do this then what will happen?" I'm a good one for playing things out in my head. Really quickly. "How will I feel if I do this?" Just in the moment. Running through my choices and discarding or saying, "Yes." And even drawing in previous experiences. It's a process of constant evaluation, and it makes a difference. So, I'd say to a methods student or a first-year teacher, "Prepare to get better."

Here is the ground floor of change, of impermanence, and in uncovering it Helen closes an important loop for me. What she calls "flexibility" is exactly what I referred to in Chapter 4 as "mindfulness, returning, attention." Flexibility is also an important part of turning pro when the going gets weird. The mental and physical disciplines that lie at the heart of flexibility are exactly the same ones that also lie at the heart of reflective practice. Helen, like the journeying Zen poet or Pirsig's selfless-climber, knows where she is and what she is doing. She knows because she bears down lightly on the moment, the movements of mind and body, the effort of attention. These are the habits of practice and mind that define and renew, that make living the teacher's life possible. Understood this way, Helen's struggle to be flexible, to live in the center of change, to operate on the basis of moment-by-moment mindfulness, becomes as much a form of meditation as an academic exercise. This teaching meditation is not the same as the varied forms of spiritual meditation. Yet, the teacher in the classroom—no less than the monk or nun praying in the cloister or chanting in the zendo, caring for the sick, or working in the fields—is staying on the journey, continually returning to attention, the beginning, home, where each moment we are reborn.

When you arrive at this place, you will know it, because it has been near at hand all along.

Epilogue

In Chapter 4 I mentioned Nancie Atwell, the Maine middle school teacher. In the early 1980s she experienced an epiphany of sorts that led her to begin living her life as a teacher in a way that integrated professional practice with personal life and language. In 1987 she chronicled these changes in a best-selling book titled *In the Middle,* which, I would say, over the last ten years has caused more reform in the teaching of language arts in this country than all the educational research and scholarship combined. It was a hell of a book, and I have been grateful to be able to use it as a text in my methods classes.

This year, when I went to order books for the following semester, I discovered that Atwell has written a second edition. I got my examination copy of the new version of *In the Middle* in the mail the other day, and I find myself even more admiring of the author than I was before. This second edition is not like some other second editions of successful books, which might rework dated material and add a new chapter or two. For Atwell, revising her book turned out to be a real occasion to return to the roots of her teaching and writing practice, and to begin her teaching life all over again. Section One, for example, is titled "Always Beginning" and opens with an epigraph from Rilke:

> If the angel deigns to come, it will be because you have
> convinced him, not by your tears, but by your humble resolve
> to be always beginning.

Later on in that same section Atwell writes:

> Teaching writing as a process gave me permission to view teaching as
> a process too. From my writing I gained the courage to change my
> mind and my life and the humility to revise my practice whenever ex-
> perience teaches me there's something else I can do to help kids be-
> come stronger, smarter, more purposeful. And so, ten years later, I
> turn to the next clean page and begin again.

That's really what it's all about, isn't it? Once we really begin, there is no end to it, and nothing remains the same. If we want to stay on the journey we need to make the journey itself home, and forget about ever finally arriving somewhere. The only way to do that is each day, each page, each moment, begin again. Even though Atwell has never heard about them, she understands the Fundamental Principle and the Four Pillars as well as anyone ever could.

Right now I am fifty years old. The bird dog my student gave me so long ago has been dead three years, the same amount of time I have been working on this book, which is now finished. Where to go now? Along with Atwell, along with all the other teachers out there who are trying to find and then stay on their ways, I take up the search for a beginning. It is not easy. I need guides, guides like Frank, who, when I asked him what he admired most in his colleagues, replied without hesitation, "I admire the risk takers, the ones who aren't afraid to get out of the box." I follow guides like Helen, who used to be my student, but is now my teacher. She teaches me that the mind every teacher needs is not only the mind that knows itself as it flows through each day and year, but it is also the mind that can recognize its own ignorance and delusion and still reach for greater and deeper understanding, the mind that naturally keeps learning.

And I follow Amanda who, in answering the same question I put to Frank, said:

> The quality I admire most is that possessed by the people who still continue to learn. I know that teachers are so busy and they have so many papers to do and they have families so that there's very little time. But I don't see any choice. That's just something you have to do, to do the job well. And the teachers I respect most, and the ones I think are most alive, are still learning something. They are curious; they're voracious readers. The guy teaching in the room next to me is a good example. You loan him a book, and he brings it back the next day, and he's read it, and he's all fired up about it, and he's constantly searching for something new, and he's got a great mind. He's not bored, and therefore he's not boring. To be a teacher I think you have to be bright and complicated in this way.

I want to be that guy. I have a long way to go.

Works Cited

Atwell, Nancie. 1987. *In the Middle: Reading and Learning with Adolescents.* Portsmouth, NH: Boynton/Cook.

———. 1998. *In the Middle: New Understandings About Writing, Reading, and Learning.* 2d ed. Portsmouth, NH: Boynton/Cook.

Basho. [1689] 1986. *Back Roads to Far Towns: Basho's Oku-No-Hosomichi.* Trans. Cid Corman and Kamaike Susumu. Fredonia, NY: White Pine Press.

Browne, Thomas. [1643] 1937. "Religio Medici." In *The Harvard Classics,* ed. Charles W. Eliot, 249–332. New York: P. F. Collier & Son.

Collom, Jack. 1985. *Moving Windows: Evaluating the Poetry Children Write.* New York: Teachers & Writers Collaborative.

Cuban, Larry. 1993. *How Teachers Taught: Constancy and Change in American Classrooms, 1880–1990.* 2d ed. New York: Teachers College Press.

Dewey, John. [1938] 1975. *Experience and Education.* New York: Collier Books.

Dogen, Eihei. [1243] 1985a. "Actualizing the Fundamental Point." In *Moon in a Dewdrop: Writings of Zen Master Dogen,* ed. K. Tanahashi, trans. D. Welch and K. Tanahashi, 69–73. San Francisco: North Point Press.

———. [1243] 1985b. "Guidelines for Studying the Way." In *Moon in a Dewdrop: Writings of Zen Master Dogen,* ed. K. Tanahashi, trans. D. Welch and K. Tanahashi, 31–43. San Francisco: North Point Press.

Dogen, Eihei, and Kosho Uchiyama. [1243] 1985. "Rules for Zazen." In *Moon in a Dewdrop: Writings of Zen Master Dogen,* ed. K. Tanahashi, trans. D. Welch and K. Tanahashi, 30–31. San Francisco: North Point Press.

Dudley-Marling, Curt. 1997. *Living With Uncertainty: The Messy Reality of Classroom Practice.* Portsmouth, NH: Heinemann.

Emerson, Ralph Waldo. [1841] 1966. "Self Reliance." In *The Romantic Movement in American Writing,* ed. Richard Harter Fogle, 40–57. New York: The Odyssey Press.

Fish, Stanley. 1989. *Doing What Comes Naturally: Change, Rhetoric, and the Practice of Theory in Literary and Legal Studies.* Durham, NC: Duke University Press.

Freire, Paulo. [1970] 1992. *Pedagogy of the Oppressed.* Trans. Myra Bergman Ramos. New York: Continuum.

Fry, Northrup. 1963. *Fables of Identity: Studies in Poetic Mythology.* New York: Harcourt, Brace, and World Co.

Gere, Ann Ruggles, Colleen Fairbanks, Alan Howes, Laura Roop, and David Schaafsma. 1992. *Language and Reflection: An Integrated Approach to Teaching English.* New York: Macmillan.

Hudson-Ross, Sally, and Patti McWhorter. 1995. "Going Back/Looking in: A Teacher Educator and a High School Teacher Explore Beginning Teaching Together." *English Journal* 84: 46–54.

Kalamaras, George. 1994. *Reclaiming the Tacit Dimension: Symbolic Form in the Rhetoric of Silence.* Albany, NY: State University of New York Press.

Kapleau, Philip. 1980. *The Three Pillars of Zen.* Garden City, NJ: Anchor Books.

Katagiri, Dainin. 1982. "Introduction." In *The Zen Environment: The Impact of Zen Meditation,* xv–xvi. New York: Bantam Books.

———. 1988. *Returning to Silence: Zen Practice in Daily Life.* Boston: Shambala.

Keats, John. [1818] 1959. "To Homer." In *John Keats: Selected Poems and Letters,* ed. Douglas Bush. Boston: Houghton Mifflin.

Kinsella, W. P. 1982. *Shoeless Joe.* New York: Ballantine.

Kornfield, Jack. 1993. *A Path With Heart.* New York: Bantam Books.

Kutz, Eleanor. 1992. "Preservice Teachers as Researchers: Developing Practice and Creating Theory in the English Classroom." *English Education* 24: 67–76.

Langer, Ellen. 1989. *Mindfulness.* Reading, MA: Addison-Wesley.

Lao Tsu. 1972. *Tao Te Ching.* Trans. Gia-Fu Feng and Jane English. New York: Vintage Books.

Mayher, John. 1990. *Uncommon Sense: Theoretical Practice in Language Education.* Portsmouth, NH: Boynton/Cook.

Moffett, James. 1994. *The Universal Schoolhouse: Spiritual Awakening Through Education.* San Francisco: Jossey-Bass.

Moffett, James, and Betty Jane Wagner. 1983. *Student-Centered Language Arts and Reading, K–13: A Handbook for Teachers.* 3d ed. Boston: Houghton-Mifflin.

Mountain, Marian. 1982. *The Zen Environment: The Impact of Zen Meditation.* New York: Bantam Books.

Nhat Hanh, Thich. [1975] 1987. *The Miracle of Mindfulness: A Manual on Meditation.* Boston: Beacon Press.

———. 1990. *Transformation and Healing: Sutra on the Four Establishments of Mindfulness.* Berkeley, CA: Parallax Press.

North, Stephen. 1987. *The Making of Knowledge in Composition: Portrait of an Emerging Field.* Portsmouth, NH: Boynton/Cook.

Pagels, Elaine. 1989. *The Gnostic Gospels.* New York: Vintage Books.

Pirsig, Robert M. [1974] 1976. *Zen & the Art of Motorcycle Maintenance: An Inquiry into Values.* New York: Bantam Books.

Plato. 1961a. "Phaedo." In *The Collected Dialogues of Plato*, eds. Edith Hamilton and Huntington Cairns, trans. H. Trendennick, 40–98. Princeton, NJ: Princeton University Press.

———. 1961b. "Phaedrus." In *The Collected Dialogues of Plato*, eds. Edith Hamilton and Huntington Cairns, trans. R. Hackforth, 475–525. Princeton, NJ: Princeton University Press.

Ritchie, Joy S., and David E. Wilson. 1993. "Dual Apprenticeships: Subverting and Supporting Critical Teaching." *English Education* 25(2): 67–83.

Schon, Donald A. 1983. *The Reflective Practitioner: How Professionals Think in Action.* New York: Basic Books.

———. 1987. *Educating the Reflective Practitioner: Toward a New Design for Teaching and Learning in the Professions.* San Francisco: Jossey-Bass.

Smagorinsky, Peter, and Melissa E. Whiting. 1995. *How English Teachers Get Taught: Methods of Teaching the Methods Class.* Urbana, IL: National Council of Teachers of English.

Suzuki, Daisetz T. 1960. *Manual of Zen Buddhism.* New York: Grove Press.

———. [1970] 1989. *Zen and Japanese Culture.* Princeton, NJ: Princeton University Press.

Suzuki, Shunryu. 1970. *Zen Mind, Beginner's Mind: Informal Talks on Zen Meditation and Practice.* New York: Weatherhill.

Tanahashi, Kazuaki. 1985. "Introduction." In *Moon in a Dewdrop: Writings of Zen Master Dogen*, ed. K. Tanahashi. San Francisco: North Point Press.

Tinberg, Howard. 1991. "An Enlargement of Observation: More on Theory Building in Composition." *College Composition and Communication* 42: 36–44.

Tremmel, Robert. 1991. *Driving the Milford Blacktop.* Kansas City, MO: BkMk Press.

———. 1993. "Zen and the Art of Reflective Practice in Teacher Education." *Harvard Educational Review* 63: 434–88.

———. 1993–94. "I Read Two Articles in the Paper This Morning." *Poetry Northwest* 34 (Winter): 12.

Uchiyama, Kosho. 1993. *Opening the Hand of Thought: Approach to Zen*, ed. Carey Warner, trans. Shohaku Okumura and Tom Wright. New York: Arkana.

Vinz, Ruth. 1996. *Composing a Teacher's Life.* Portsmouth, NH: Boynton/Cook.

Yasutani, Hakuun. 1996. *Flowers Fall: A Commentary on Zen Master Dogen's Genjokoan.* Boston: Shambala.

Yokoi, Yuho, with Daizen Victoria. 1990. *Zen Master Dogen: An Introduction with Selected Writings.* New York: Weatherhill.